GLOBAL CAMPAIGN FOR WOMEN'S HUMAN RIGHTS

AN Das

MD PUBLICATIONS PVT LTD
NEW DELHI
www.mdppl.com

Published by:

MD Publications Pvt Ltd
"MD House", 11, Darya Ganj,
New Delhi - 110 002
Phone : +91-11-45355555
E-mail : contact@mdppl.com
website : www.mdppl.com

ISBN: 978-81-7533-297-3

Published and Printed by Mr. Pranav Gupta on behalf of **MD Publications Pvt Ltd** at JJ offset Printers, Delhi.

GLOBAL CAMPAIGN FOR WOMEN'S HUMAN RIGHTS

PREFACE

The term "women's human rights" and the set of practices that accompanies its use are the continuously evolving product of an international movement to improve the status of women. In the 1980s and 1990s, women's movements around the world formed networks and coalitions to give greater visibility both to the problems that women face every day and to the centrality of women's experiences in economic, social, political and environmental issues. In the evolution of what is becoming a global women's movement, the term "women's human rights" has served as a locus for praxis, that is, for the development of political strategies shaped by the interaction between analytical insights and concrete political practices. Further, the critical tools, the concerted activism, and the broad-based international networks that have grown up around movements for women's human rights have become a vehicle for women to develop the political skills necessary for the twenty-first century.

The concept of women's human rights owes its success and the proliferation of its use to the fact that it is simultaneously prosaic and revolutionary. On the one hand, the idea of women's human rights makes common sense. It declares, quite simply, that as human beings women have human rights. Anyone would find her or himself hard-pressed to publicly make and defend the contrary argument that women are not human. So in many ways, the claim that women have human rights seems quite ordinary. On the other hand, "women's human rights" is a revolutionary notion. This radical reclamation of humanity and the corollary insistence that women's rights are human rights have profound transformative potential. The incorporation of women's perspectives and lives into human rights' standards and practice forces recognition of the dismal failure of countries worldwide to accord women the human dignity and respect that they deserve-simply as human beings.

Women's rights around the world are an important indicator of understanding global well-being. Many may think that women's rights are only an issue in countries where religion is law, such as many Muslim countries. Discussions of human rights often fail to acknowledge the unique concerns of women around the globe particularly as they relate to the subordination of and injustices against women. Yet clearly, women's rights are human rights' concerns. Violence against women and girls is the most pervasive violation of human rights in the world today. Discrimination against women and girls is an important basic cause of malnutrition. The very high rates of child malnutrition and low birth weight throughout much of South Asia are linked to such factors as women's poor access to education and their low levels of participation in paid employment, compared with other regions.

I am very grateful to Mr. Pranav Gupta, Director of MD Publications Pvt Ltd, New Delhi, for his kind cooperation and support for this book.

AN Das

Contents

1

Global Campaign for Women's Human Rights

An Introduction

The 1998 Global Campaign for Women's Human Rights was launched by the Center for Women's Global Leadership, in collaboration with hundreds of organizations worldwide, with the theme Celebrate and Demand Women's Human Rights. In 1998, the world commemorated the 50th anniversary of the *Universal Declaration of Human Rights (UDHR)*. The *UDHR* enshrines far-reaching principles of human dignity with the proclamation that "all human beings are born free and equal in dignity and rights," and the stipulation that human rights apply to all equally without distinction of any kind including sex. Unfortunately, documentation of human rights abuses in 1998 illustrates all too clearly that the bold sentiments of the *UDHR* have not been effectively translated into concrete protection. The campaign had three primary goals: visibility, accountability and action. First, it sought to ensure that human rights abuses against women remained at the forefront of public attention throughout the year. Second, it used this global focus on human rights to demand the accountability of governments and the UN to their human rights obligations to women. Finally, it framed each of these in the context of action, as in the campaign slogan "take action to make it happen."

The 1998 Global Campaign sought to translate the rhetoric of world conference agreements and human right treaties into concrete demands and strategies as well as tools and opportunities for women's human right's advocacy. In consultation with a wide range of women's human rights advocates throughout the world, a Take Action kit was developed to facilitate public education, advocacy and mobilization directed toward a variety of arenas. The material in the kit included five demands, two postcard actions, a poster, and background information to link the demands to advocacy activities utilizing the *UDHR*, the *Vienna Declaration and Programme of Action* and the *Beijing Declaration and Platform for Action*.

The demands, the poster, the postcards, and the kit were distributed widely throughout the world and disseminated in March 1998 in New York at the UN Commission on the Status of Women and in Geneva at the Commission on Human Rights. A Campaign website was developed and featured an online version of the kit as well as space for exchange of messages and information about events. From Buenos Aires to Bucharest, Nairobi and New Delhi, women throughout the world participated in diverse ways, adapting the campaign themes and materials in a manner appropriate to their own goals and context.

The Campaign culminated with two major events around December 10: a Global Tribunal, with the theme "Celebrate and Demand" and an international solidarity activity, "Women Light the Way for Human Rights." These themes were selected to commemorate women's human rights victories, and the outstanding efforts of women's human rights movements around the world. At the same time, they focused a "spotlight" on the continuing violations of women's human rights that take place in massive numbers everywhere.

The Global Tribunal, held on December 9, 1998 in New York City included:

Testimonies from other tribunals held in 1998: from Zimbabwe, the denial of full property rights to women and from Costa Rica, the mistreatment of women workers and the abuse of their right to work in a safe and healthy environment; successes achieved by women's human rights movements: the passage of CEDAW as a local ordinance in San Francisco/USA, the inclusion of gender issues won by the Women's Caucus for Gender Justice in the International Criminal Court, and the incorporation of a broad anti-discrimination clause including gender, race and sexual orientation into the new South African Constitution; and stories reflecting issues that women have identified as human rights crises requiring far greater attention: trafficking from Central and Eastern Europe, gender apartheid and the systematic abuse of women in Afghanistan, and domestic violence and the particular obstacles faced by immigrant women survivors of domestic violence as they seek justice through the courts in New York City.

The Tribunal was followed by a local Women Light the Way event. This was a multi-media vigil featuring a slide show with images of women projected onto a wall across the street from the UN. A small delegation from the tribunal met on December 10 with Mary Robinson, the High Commissioner for Human Rights, to present the results of the tribunal and the 1998 Global Campaign.

Finally, the Global Center collaborated with UNIFEM in a UN interagency exhibition, "A Life Free of Violence Against Women," in the visitor's lobby of the UN in New York as part of the 16 Days of Activism Against Gender Violence campaign. The items displayed by the Global Center included posters and postcards received from women around the world with messages and images on the theme "Imagine a World Where All Women Enjoy Their Human Rights."

1998 AROUND THE WORLD

Last year, the Global Center received information on a myriad of activities coordinated by individuals and organizations from around the world for the 1998 Global Campaign for Women's Human Rights, 16 Days of Activism Against Gender Violence, and Women Light the Way for Human Rights. For example, Tribunals were held in at least 15 countries, including Barbados, Bolivia, Cameroon, Fiji, Kenya, and Poland.

Many individuals and organizations filled out both postcards in the Take Action kit - both paper copies and on-line. A number of organizations also produced their own adaptations of postcards addressed to local and national officials - in Argentina, Australia, Croatia, Serbia, the Netherlands, Nigeria and Poland, among others.

Organizations developed posters and had poster, photo and essay contests, including in Argentina, Bolivia, Costa Rica, Mauritius, Nigeria, and Peru.

A wide range of organizations also participated in the Women Light the Way activities, both by sending messages to the Global Center to be delivered to the High Commissioner for Human Rights and by incorporating the theme of "light" into their activities. For example, in Ahmedabad, India, a meeting of grassroots women was held which included a lamp lighting ceremony in support of "Women Light the Way." Similar activities were held in Armenia, Ireland, Japan, the Philippines, and the USA, among others.

Descriptions of these activities can be found in the Latin America and Caribbean Women's Health Journal.

In 1998, UNIFEM launched a series of UN Inter-Agency Regional Campaigns to Eliminate Violence Against Women in Latin America and the Caribbean, Africa, and in Asia and the Pacific. With the overall theme, "A Life Free of Violence...It's Our Right," the campaigns shared three goals: raising public awareness about violence against women as a violation of human rights; celebrating women's rights achievements; and bringing together the efforts of the UN system on this issue in a coordinated manner. The regional campaigns are continuing in 1999.

As part of the regional Campaign in Asia and the Pacific, 40,000 copies of the poster "Our Rights: Women's rights related to police," were produced in 14 official languages and distributed to police stations throughout India. UNIFEM is also assisting the Police Training Institute there to develop a curriculum on violence against women that will become a compulsory course for all police officers.

THE GLOBAL CAMPAIGN FOR WOMEN'S HUMAN RIGHTS

International conferences commonly adopt the title of their host cities. Thus, Beijing now refers to the United Nations Fourth World Conference on Women in 1995; and Cairo no longer only signifies a city in Egypt, but also symbolizes the 1994 International Conference on Population and Development. Vienna, in this case, refers to the 1993 United Nations World Conference on Human Rights. In anticipation of this Conference, the Center for Women's Global Leadership helped to form an international movement of women called the Global Campaign for Women's Human Rights ("Global Campaign") in an effort to bring gender-specific violations of women's human rights to the forefront of international human rights discourse. At the core of the campaign was the idea that women should organize locally to affect global issues and to understand better the relationship of local issues and actions to international policy. In the wake of the Vienna Conference, the grassroots women's movement was called upon to influence global human rights policy both at the national and international levels.

At the Vienna Conference, the Global Campaign made demands in two principal areas. A petition signed by more than half a million people around the world exemplified the critical nature of these demands. First, the petition called for the integration of women throughout the agenda of the Vienna Conference. This meant that every human rights issue on the agenda was to include a consideration of its specific effects on women. A discussion about refugee policy or political prisoners, for example, would also examine the particular experiences of women in those situations. Second, the Global Campaign demanded that the Vienna Conference recognize gender-based violence against women as an international human rights abuse. Despite the reality that this problem affects women in every country around the world, the issue had been left out of the human rights agenda. This omission demonstrates the degree to which women's human rights have gone unrecognized in the world, and emphasizes the need to expand the mainstream human rights movement to embrace issues pertaining specifically to women.

The final Conference document acknowledged and addressed most of the Global Campaign's Demands. The Vienna Declaration and Programme of Action formally recognized the specific human rights concerns of women. It stressed both the need to address particular women's human rights issues, such as gender-based violence, and the integration of gender perspectives into other areas of human rights activity. This was an important catalyst in the effort to make women's human rights visible.

A closer look at the Vienna Declaration, however, reveals that it is easier to achieve recognition of women's human rights in specific sections of the document than it is to integrate women and gender-conscious perspectives throughout the document and the entire process. This revelation poses one of our challenges for the future: we have successfully exposed women's issues as separate concerns, yet we are still struggling to show how women and gender issues pervade all aspects of human rights.

The impact of the Vienna Declaration on women's human rights in the United States is noteworthy in several areas. First is the recognition that violence against women, in both the public and private context, must be regarded as a human rights issue. This is critical because, prior to the Vienna Conference, violence against women was dismissed as a "private matter." The public/private distinction serves to diminish the significance of women's issues. One method of abolishing the distinction is to show that what is often termed "private," in fact has public implications. The intended effect would be to render the distinction artificial. By putting violence against women on the public agenda, we also begin to understand the true nature of the public's responsibility for what happens in the so-called "private" sphere.

Implementation is the next stage. We have successfully

persuaded the United Nations to appoint a Special Rapporteur on Violence Against Women, to begin the process of documenting and interpreting the meaning of violence against women and the ways in which international conventions and instruments can be used to address the issue.

The next step is to learn how to document more substantially the ways in which this violence occurs. Improved documentation will help us to establish the connection between gender-based violence and traditional human rights concepts.

Furthermore, we need to promote the concept that individual states share the responsibility to confront women's human rights issues, particularly violence against women. This duty may be analogized to the treatment of slavery as a human rights issue. It is generally understood that the state bears responsibility for preventing slavery, even though the state does not actually practice it. The practice of slavery may properly be classified as a "private" activity whereby individual citizens deprive others of their freedom. The severity of the situation, however, forces governments to acknowledge their obligation to interfere with that "private" relationship and to declare slavery an unacceptable practice that violates human rights. Much of our discussion on violence against women bears a resemblance to the condition of slavery. Both practices may be deemed "private," yet individual citizens, as well as the state, have a measure of control over what occurs in the private sphere. This is not a novel idea, but simply a question of who decides what type of behavior is acceptable. Understanding this notion contributes to building the political will that denounces this kind of violence in our lives and in our communities, both at the local and state levels. To achieve a successful turnaround we have to reexamine the ways women's human rights have been categorized and dismissed as a "private" matter.

Another topic that deserves attention is the Convention on the Elimination of All Forms of Discrimination Against Women ("CEDAW"). The Vienna Conference called for the ratification of CEDAW and encouraged countries that had already ratified CEDAW to commence with its full-scale implementation. The United States should now ponder what it means to be one of the few countries in the world, and the only industrialized nation, that has not ratified CEDAW. What does it mean for this country to say it is in favor of human rights, but then to fail to ratify the International Convention on the Elimination of all Forms of Racial Discrimination, the International Covenant on Economic, Social and Cultural Rights, and CEDAW? This inactivity will considerably impede the advancement of domestic human rights.

We also need to look at the resources provided for the implementation of women's human rights, as compared to those offered to promote other human rights issues. Why has this been sidelined by human rights organizations, the United Nations, and our governments? The State Department of the United States, for example, generated a great deal of publicity in its 1994 Human Rights Report by covering specific abuses against women. A close examination of actual foreign policy reveals that there is nothing contained therein which reflects the findings in the report. So women's human rights issues are in the report, but the government does not take those findings into account when formulating actual policy matters. This should alert people that women's concerns are not yet receiving serious consideration, either at the resource level or at the policy-making level.

The other challenge from the Vienna Conference is to integrate women throughout human rights theory and practice. In many ways this is much more difficult, due to the public's unwillingness to concede that unique women's perspectives exist for a number of different issues. Female refugees, for example, are often treated differently from male refugees. Without commenting on the relative severity of this treatment, we must investigate and analyze these conditions, often thought to be universal, both in terms of gender considerations and in terms of racial, ethnic, and cultural considerations. In addition, we need to examine the specific way that various populations experience disparate treatment and implement policies to correct them.

Another human rights challenge for us is to create a scheme for bringing human rights issues home and applying them within the United States. One of the big challenges of the Vienna Conference is to convince Americans that women's human rights is not only an international question, but also must be understood and evaluated as a matter of domestic concern. Human rights violations exist in the United States on two levels. The first tier deals with the ways in which people within this country are violated, such as how women, racial minorities, indigenous people, gays and lesbians, and immigrants are subjected to abuse on a daily basis. The second tier addresses how the United States government plays a role in human rights abuses occurring in other parts of the world.

A viable international human rights movement must assume responsibility for monitoring not only what other governments do, but also what our own governments do. In doing so, we will find the basis for a true international solidarity movement. Solidarity happens when we become accountable for domestic government, and then ascertain how our government should collaborate with others to eliminate human rights abuses worldwide. From a gender-conscious perspective, this is the best way to expand the current human rights movement into a truly global movement. With some effort, this perspective will help us to realize the important mission of connecting international human rights with domestic movements in the United States.

PERSPECTIVE ON WOMEN AND INTERNATIONAL HUMAN RIGHTS AFTER THE VIENNA DECLARATION

For the first time ever, violations of women's human rights were specifically recognized by the United Nations at its World Conference on Human Rights in June 1993. The final Declaration and Vienna Declaration that arose out of the Vienna conference ("the Vienna Declaration") specifically recognizes "the human rights of women" as "an inalienable, integral and indivisible part of universal human rights," presses for "the eradication of all forms of discrimination against women, both hidden and overt," and demands that "The equal status of women and the human rights of women... be integrated into the mainstream of United Nations system-wide activity." At the urging of an international coalition of women's advocates, the Vienna Declaration also specifically condemns "gender-based violence and all forms of sexual harassment and exploitation," calls upon the General Assembly "to adopt a draft declaration on violence against women," and "welcomes the decision of the Commission on Human Rights to consider the appointment of a special rapporteur on violence against women."

Vienna marks a milestone in the efforts to gain recognition of women's human rights. Until recently the very notion that women could have a claim to distinct and legally cognizable human rights was virtually unheard of in mainstream international dialogue. Nor had a United Nations World Conference on Human Rights ever before recognized gender-based violence as a human rights concern. This recognition greatly advances recent efforts by women's human rights advocates to distinguish between those human rights abuses that occur in the public sphere, and therefore predominantly affect men, and those in the private realm which are largely targeted against women. The Vienna Declaration has the potential to serve as a catalyst in leading the way toward further United Nations action. Thus, its very existence represents an enormous accomplishment.

Yet Vienna's success remains limited. The final document, despite its own demands that women be "integrated" into the activities of the United Nations, continues to marginalize and isolate women's concerns. For example, it fails to add the word "women" whenever "race" or other forms of oppression are mentioned, instead grouping "women's issues" in separate, specially designated sections. Thus, women experiencing complex, interwoven oppressions - not based on gender alone and not simply "additive" - still have no formal language to express their claims. For example, they may be able to argue that their human rights have been denied because they are a racial, national or ethnic, religious, or linguistic minority, an indigenous person, a migrant worker, a child, a disabled person, and/or a woman. But, they cannot gain recognition of their claim based on an intertwining of these factors, such as violations committed against a woman because she is a Spanish speaking, Latina migrant worker or a woman living under Muslim laws.

A broad-based and loosely defined coalition of women's groups has been organizing internationally to tackle this dilemma, and ensure inclusion of women's human rights on the Vienna agenda and beyond. To combat the tendency of the mainstream human rights community to separate out, and in the process minimize, women's concerns, or alternatively, to ignore them altogether, the coalition leaders adopted a two-pronged approach, which was implemented nationally, regionally, and internationally before the Vienna Conference and at Vienna itself. They developed a comprehensive body of separate women's demands through the myriad of women's activities, emphasizing why women's rights are human rights. They pushed for inclusion and integration of women's issues into the broader human rights agenda by participating in the working groups of officially recognized non-governmental organizations, which met to formulate and articulate positions on human rights issues, both before and during the Vienna conference, to present to the official U.N. body for its consideration in its final document. In addition, they lobbied the official U.N. delegations at the World Conference, directly and intensively, issue by issue, country by country.

Still, even though women's concerns were brought up in substantive working groups and made their way onto some preliminary drafts of the Vienna Declaration, the drafters of the final, official document failed to integrate women's concerns throughout. This chapter seeks to review one essential aspect of the approach taken in Vienna: the decision to focus on acts of violence against women as the principle human rights concern. This strategy illustrates the painstaking efforts many women throughout the world have taken to change the face of international human rights discourse. Like any strategy, as illustrated in the first section below, it has its benefits and limitations. And like any strategy, it developed out of a range of experiences both before and during Vienna, that influenced the thinking on what would best accomplish the dual goals of fully integrating women's human rights concerns in all aspects of human rights discourse while calling for the strengthening of existing mechanisms, and the creation of new ones, that address the specific gender-based human rights violations experienced by women. While admitting the limitations of this strategy, this essay endorses the basic, yet potentially transformative, premise that international human rights dialogue must be opened to include the diverse voices of women experiencing a broad range of human rights abuses.

USING VIOLENCE AS A FOCAL POINT FOR RAISING WOMEN'S HUMAN RIGHTS

The success in Vienna in getting the United Nations even to recognize women's human rights at all can be traced in significant measure to the decision of the organizing coalition to focus on violence against women as a key issue in advancing women's human rights. This concentration on acts of violence against women grew, in part, out of the experiences and efforts of women around the world. As women in different countries and regions have focused their attention in recent years on violence against women, an important realization was made over and over again. Across cultures and throughout time, societies view violence against women in the private sphere as something apart from, and less egregious than, violence that occurs in the public sphere. The traditional notions of human rights abuses have evolved with the distinction that abuses in the private sphere occur most frequently against women and those in the public sphere occur most frequently against men. Examples of the private sphere abuses against women include intimate violence, rape, genital mutilation, and dowry murders. Examples of the public sphere abuses committed frequently against men are torture, arbitrary detention, disappearances, and summary executions. The private sphere abuses have not previously aroused public outcry or protection to the same degree as public sphere violence.

As this awareness crystallized in the minds of women throughout the world, a common understanding emerged in the work of women advocating for women's rights protection. Violence against women has been segmented and sequestered out of the public discourse on human rights, just as its occurrence has been kept hidden from public scrutiny. At the same time, the prevailing view of the "public sphere" was that the most commonly perpetuated acts of violence against women, such as rape and sexual assault, had been minimized if not outright ignored.

This realization led women's human rights advocates to a twofold belief. First, violence against women in its many forms is so widely practiced, universally condoned, rarely punished, and at the same time so pernicious, pervasive and immobilizing that no meaningful human rights program could fail to address it. Second, the prohibition, protection, and punishment of violence against women were something upon which virtually all women, from all walks of life around the globe could agree on. This in turn led women's rights advocates to make violence against women the focal point at the Vienna Human Rights Convention. Moreover, the widely-publicized rapes in the former Yugoslavia had done much to catapult the issue of violence against women into the international human rights arena, thus giving a very public and recent "platform" upon which to build in Vienna.

This narrow strategy helped guarantee advancement for women's human rights at Vienna. First, media around the world carried the common message that women in Vienna demanded an end to gender-based violence. Second, a singular drive helped solidify the push for a U.N. special rapporteur to investigate violence against women. Third, a uniform and global outcry against gender-based violence helped magnify the message's impact on both international policy makers and international human rights groups. Fourth, a strong, united push on the issue of violence placed it prominently in the final document of the World Conference.

Still, this strategy, for all its political mileage, also carried limitations. By focusing narrowly on acts of violence against women, other issues of grave concern to women, including literacy, poverty, gender segregation, discriminatory divorce, and citizenship laws, were effectively excluded. In turn, the media exacerbated this problem by presenting the most simplistic, sensationalized accounts of women's concerns. Thus, both conference attenders and non-attenders were left with the impression that women's human rights violations only concerned acts of violence. Those issues not directly linked with violence, nor demanding an in-depth examination of the causes and consequences of the violence, seemed silenced and ignored.

Women from developing countries, women who did not participate in the planning coalition and women who had come seeking a receptive audience for addressing their concerns regarding development, literacy, religious freedom, and other issues, found no locus of support. Instead they were met with isolation, frustration, and to some extent disempowerment.

In turn, many of those women from "North" or "South," who were involved in the pre- conference preparations, missed a rare opportunity to engage in genuine dialogue with women otherwise rarely seen or heard from, i.e., women who are not world travellers, women who do not attend the feminist conferences and international planning sessions, women who are struggling in their own countries, their own communities, in their own lives, to impact the profound ways in which sexism, racism, neo-colonialism, and monetary greed affect their lives. Although some women were able to find space and time to talk to each other in the lounges, corridors, and coffee shops, there were few formalized channels in which to broaden the exchange of perspectives, issues, concerns, and values in order to further the building of a multicultural, multi-ethnic, multi-economic global network addressing women's concerns. The principal accomplishment of Vienna was the establishment of a firm foothold which allows for issues of violence against women to be treated as human rights violations in the mainstream international arena.

In particular, the breakdown of the public/private dichotomy in examining violence against women represents a formidable accomplishment. Two pivotal events occurred in Vienna which catapulted the issue of violence against women into the eye of the public and of the United Nations First, a day-long "Global Tribunal on Violations of Women's Human Rights" provided a forum for female survivors of violence and their advocates - drawn from around the world and from a diverse array of experiences - to tell their own stories.

Second, representatives of several women's organizations addressed the plenary session of the United Nations, on a broad range of issues of concern to women, thus speaking directly to the power brokers who are so often out of reach in the General Assembly. Both the Global Tribunal and the presentations to the U.N. General Assembly sharply raised issues of violence as well as issues of power, structural adjustment and development, and other social, cultural and economic human rights issues which profoundly affect women and their quality of life throughout the world.

Yet the result of Vienna was to cast a blinding spotlight on issues of violence while ignoring other pressing issues. This occurred despite efforts taken to ensure integration of women's rights in every aspect of human rights, and to strengthen existing mechanisms and create new ones to focus on the human rights violations that specifically affect women. This tension between striving for a broad, comprehensive view of women's human rights while concentrating on the most salient and compelling issue - violence against women - raises the broader problem facing women working to enhance the human rights protection of women: how to work effectively within a hierarchical, complex, and constraining system without being corrupted by that system; or how to play the game and break the rules at the same time while moving forward with these efforts, activists and scholars alike must vigilantly avoid traps laid by the "powers that be" to veer us off our course. In fighting for a broad definition of human rights for women, we are fighting a battle on at least two fronts. The first hurdle, and the one mightily surmounted in Vienna, is gaining world attention for the rights of women as human rights. The long-standing second hurdle is to raise the stature of the so-called "second generation" human rights (i.e., social, cultural, and economic rights), to a level of high priority in the world community.

To keep the women's human rights agenda intact and focused, we must be ever watchful that the issues of importance to women - issues such as development, literacy, and poverty - are not lost in the struggle to gain protection from the most visible and most obviously detrimental abuses that entail violence. In the next part of this essay, we postulate how to accomplish this through the application of an old concept - an "inside/outside" construct - with a new twist.

AN INSIDE/OUTSIDE CONSTRUCT

Theorists "on the outside" of oppression have long been most visible in the theorizing about, and to a lesser extent, in the organizing around, international human rights. This gives rise to the danger that those actually experiencing the abuses discussed are not included in the process of theoretical development. When this occurs, the voices of those with the sharpest perspective on what constitutes human rights abuses, and of those with firsthand knowledge about the direct and daily effects of perceived oppressions in the world, are silenced. Consequently, the mainstream discourse on human rights becomes an intellectual theoretical debate, rather than one which grapples with the actual, complex dimensions of human experience. Whether tacitly or explicitly, the official international human rights mechanisms and power structure fosters, and even encourages, an intellectual assessment removed from human experience. The more distant and removed the point of reference, the easier it is to dismantle, make divisible, compartmentalize, segregate, minimize, dismiss, and even ignore the full dimensionality and impact of human rights abuses. We call this the "outsider" view - human rights abuses fall "outside" the sphere of the daily life of those theorizing, discussing, and formulating solutions about them, at least in attitude if not in actual fact. Nowhere is this more consistent with the unwritten agenda to keep the powerless and disenfranchised hidden and unheard than in the realm of women's human rights.

For those experiencing the oppression of human rights abuses, the issues present an indivisible, experiential whole. Their experiences are not readily fragmented into neat compartments. They cannot be dismissed or ignored. They color the entirety of the life of the person experiencing the abuse. And this is particularly true for women, who are most likely to suffer a broader range of abuses in their lives with fewer resources, recourse, or redress. In working within a system that tolerates and often endorses the ranking of human rights issues, which privileges some while excluding or trivializing others, women's human rights activists must consistently fight against the impulses or propulsions towards similar behavior.

Women working to build global, broad-based women's human rights agenda are on the "inside." This inside approach works toward a comprehensive and integrative approach to women and human rights; one that is rooted in the actual experiences of women. Among women, however, there are degrees of "insiderness." Those closest to the experience, with firsthand knowledge of state policies, social or cultural customs, discriminatory practices, or economic deprivations that endorse or perpetuate their continued subordination, will have the clearest perspective on what constitutes human rights abuses against women, where they occur, and how. These voices are essential to the theoretical development of women's human rights discourse. Without their participation and leadership, theoretical development is the net loser.

The standpoint of the oppressed gives rise not only to a different epistemological position, but to one that is advantageous. It provides the basis for an arguably more impartial view of reality that comes closer to representing the interests of society as a whole. Alternatively, whereas the standpoint of the dominant group reflects the needs of only one sector of the population.

An "inside/outside" construct can be used to examine tensions between outsiders and insiders who theorize about gender and human rights. In the "outsider" approach, development of human rights theories evolves from a limited range of participants examining the issue. Outsiders focus their inquiry on individual acts that may constitute human rights abuses. This is combined with an attempt to isolate, but not link, the various inter-related factors that cause or contribute to the occurrence of the abuse.

In contrast, using the "insider" approach, allows a more diverse group of women, including those women closest to the oppression at issue, to examine the problem and to define it. For "insiders," the focus of the inquiry tends to be not only on the specific, individual acts that may constitute the human rights violation, but also on the complex, material circumstances and power imbalances that give rise to the act. Insiders also closely examine what happens after the act and the factors influencing this aftermath. This approach gains strength when it develops a gendered explanation for the abuse, rather than simply adding gender into the discussion. It uses a gender lens to create a framework which accounts for multiple, intertwined factors, such as race, class, religion, ethnicity, sexual orientation, culture, and neocolonialism that profoundly influence what is happening.

The "inside/outside" construct, as explored in this section, reflects a dynamic containing three inter-related questions: (1) who is examining the problem; (2) what is the focus of the inquiry, or how is the problem defined; and (3) what explanation is derived for what is occurring, or how the abuse is being explained.

The Question of Who

The overarching question, in moving feminist analyses and organizing strategies of human rights forward, concerns who is invited to the table. This is perhaps the most difficult aspect of the process. In order to have a truly representative table, those who are already at the table must have both initiative and resources to find and invite other voices to join them. Since the location of the gathering will strongly influence agenda-setting and the discussion process, meetings should be held in countries all over the world and particularly in places closest to the issues being raised. Once at the table, the floor must be given to those who have generally been excluded; their ideas should be respected, their priorities honored, and their views weighted determinatively in directing further development.

In making room at the table for others, we need to elucidate that our views are only representative of ourselves. To this end, we must recognize that no country is beyond reproach and examine the human rights abuses that occur in our own countries. We must examine our perspectives and our assumptions, recognize our privilege, and account for it explicitly in our work as we strive to overcome its limitations on our thinking.

The international human rights system is not designed to actually hear the voices of the oppressed. Rather, if it receives their views at all it does so in a filtered, mediated fashion, through official representatives, committees, or organizations. Women must work to maintain a broader agenda and to avoid falling prey to the limitations posed by the system itself.

In order to broaden the dialogue to include race, class, ethnicity, religion, sexuality, and culture, and the vast human rights abuses women face in their daily lives, regardless of any direct connection thereto, those with access to the table already must ensure that varied perspectives are represented. Women must be enabled to talk about their own experiences and their understandings of how the above factors meet and where they diverge. We do not deny that in order to come to an understanding of any of these issues, they must each be taken apart and examined separately. Thus, we argue that before the examination is completed, the issue must be reassembled and viewed as a whole.

A second, related difficulty concerns ensuring diverse, productive communication after the women are found and gathered at the table. "Women" do not represent a unified whole, a single perspective, and thus, we women will disagree on many issues. We may not even recognize ourselves in the experiences and perspectives of others. As Palestinian feminist Rita Giacaman reminds us: "Bridges cannot be built in a vacuum. Not every woman will agree with another woman. Sisterhood is not necessarily global." Thus, women's vocabularies, approaches, and conclusions will vary dramatically with respect to the same events. In addition, newcomers to the table will necessarily lack information from previous discussion, thus raising the dilemma of how to include them without continually repeating information and, in this sense, lowering the level of dialogue.

This problem was exemplified in Vienna, where women came from a broad range of geographic, political, economic, and cultural backgrounds, and thus disagreed with each other on many issues. Largely due to the process of politicking and lobbying at the World Conference, as well as the physical constraints of the building, the avenues of formal and informal discourse were unfortunately closed off to some women, except for the most informal "hall talk." A number of additional problems conspired against fruitful communication.

For many participants, Vienna was their first real foray into international human rights law lobbying. Some of the women were relatively new to the issue of women and human rights; in fact, the examination of human rights through a gender lens is itself a relatively new process, without a long history or established protocol. Although many women had considerable experience organizing at international and domestic conferences, never before had women organized for human rights at the level of a full United Nations World Conference on Human Rights? Because women were faced with operating within the confines of an unfamiliar bureaucratic, hierarchical, and complex system, they were pulled in various directions. Opportunities to train for effective lobbying, or develop new theories, were thereby lost.

In recognition of such problems blocking effective communication of diverse voices, women involved in organizing the 1995 World Conference on Women in Beijing have begun planning for even more extensive training and strategizing sessions than the ones held before Vienna, seeking to include a wider array of voices.

The Focus of the Inquiry

Once people are invited to the table, they must determine where to focus the inquiry. They must decide whether to define the problem as a human rights issue, and if so how. A focus on the acts themselves - the beatings, the stoning, and the rape - would neglect both the material circumstances which give rise to the acts and the consequences, far beyond treatment of bruises, leading toward further subordination of the survivor of the violation. A contextualization of the acts of abuse (*i.e.*, events that occurred before the act of violence that contributed to its commission, and events that happened after the act), is essential.

Women thinking and working in this area have long understood that violence against women is systemic, and intersects with all other aspects of their lives. Theories and plans of action have been born to address this intersection. Although the Vienna Declaration stresses acts of physical violence against women as a priority in human rights protection concerns, we should not let our future actions be misguided by that artificial limitation. Those working to expand the concept of human rights must integrate and include women and continue to address issues beyond violence itself as fundamental human rights issues which warrant the full attention, resources, and commitment of the international community.

As the Vienna conference displayed, women around the world face numerous forms of human rights violations. These violations include: acts invading women's bodily integrity, manipulating their childbearing decisions and interfering with their reproductive organs; economic exploitation, from the selling of child brides, to forced prostitution, to exclusion from development programs; assaults penalizing women for engaging in political activity in defense of themselves; so-called "domestic violence" (*i.e.*, a husband's beating/rape/torture of "his woman" in "his home"); forced compliance with restrictive gender roles, often accompanied by persecution for refusing to accept them as "appropriate" or "required" behavior; poverty; lack of educational opportunities; and the inability of women to live apart from men, or to master "men's work," such as building bridges, driving trucks, leading movements, teaching philosophy, establishing businesses, or even limitations on appearing in public without the presence of a male relative.

The Global Tribunal on Violations of Women's Human Rights at the Vienna Conference, as brilliantly conceived by an international coalition, gave women a platform, a microphone, and an audience, allowing them the freedom to tell their stories in their own voices. Each woman testified about her own experiences with violence, or about her firsthand experience trying to help another woman who could not attend because she was too scarred, too afraid, too weak to travel, or dead. Given such powerful presentations, now no one can say "it didn't happen." The Tribunal answered the fundamental question: "what is happening to women?" Yet despite efforts to address not only violence but also issues of poverty and political participation among others, it was ultimately violence that captured the attention of the media and the official U.N. body, as well as many of the non-governmental organizations in attendance. It is violence that remains in the minds of many as the central issue women want addressed.

While expanding the stage to include more voices to tell an ever widening array of stories of gender-based violence, we must simultaneously move beyond examinations of acts of violence. We need to continue to explore the roots of the violence and its deeper consequences. Gender violence, like other historical manifestations of violence, is embedded in the socioeconomic and political context of power relations. Violence against women is part of general violence found within social structures such as class, caste, religion, ethnicity, and state control - *i.e.*, structural violence. Violence against women also encompasses forms of control and coercion exercised through hierarchical and patriarchal gender relationships in the family and society. Power is at the core of violence. It runs through all human rights violations committed against women, through each of them at every stage and in every facet. Power is differently manifested and alternatively displayed, obscured, and trumpeted on women's bodies and in women's lives. Examining acts of violence alone fails to locate and explore these underlying power plays.

A feminist analysis of power is particularly persuasive when it looks beyond consequences to focus on causes. When we ask how manipulations of masculinity and femininity shape the causes, not just the effects, of militarism, then feminist analysis reveals how power works.

Thus, even if only to understand fully the violence and to locate it within a human rights framework, we need to examine the socioeconomic and political circumstances from which it emerges. As Margaret Schuler states in her groundbreaking study that undertakes such an examination, "understanding the phenomenon of gender violence requires an analysis of the patterns of violence directed toward women and the underlying mechanisms that permit the emergence and perpetuation of these patterns." We need to scrutinize the role of poverty, the militarization of society, culture, race, ethnicity, and religion in fostering, encouraging, justifying, or allowing violence against women. Close scrutiny must be given to the ways in which society reinforces violence against women through law, custom, and politics. Moreover, we must also look deeper into the aftermath of the acts to understand their impact on the individual woman, as well as on women as a group and on society as a whole. How did the woman respond? How has the violence affected her life? What recourse was available to her? What resources were available to help her cope? What social or community support was available to help her overcome the trauma? Did her relationship to the abuser affect her treatment or the receptivity of her complaints? The answers serve an important role in formulating the problem and its resolution. In turn, the formulation of both question and answer reflect whether acts of violence can be conceived as human rights violations by the society in which they occur.

Finally, in expanding our inquiry, we must move beyond an examination of how the state has either attempted to prevent the act or to respond to the act. While these questions are important, we should also "insist on asking questions about the processes by which male dominance and violence are reproduced." We must examine the social conditions that produce men who violate women, and that support, condone, or ignore the gross power imbalances, including the subjugation of women to men. How does the state tolerate or even encourage these conditions? Why? Who benefits?

Though these are hard questions, "harder questions will produce more radical answers." Merely asking these questions has already helped to dismantle the artificial, yet, until recently, unquestioned dichotomy in traditional human rights law and theory between acts that occur in the "public sphere" - things that more typically happen to men, such as torture and arbitrary detention - from those that occur in the so-called "private sphere" - things which almost exclusively affect women, such as intimate violence, rape, and other acts that are carried out by family members or by strangers, who are not state actors.

While probing further into the causes and consequences of violence, we must continue to include other issues of relevance to women. Violence, when contextualized completely, will encompass many of the social, cultural, and economic, as well as political abuses that women confront. In many instances women experience these abuses without any direct or tangible physical violence; these cases as well must continue to be raised as human rights violations.

Examining the context in which the violence occurs will inescapably reveal the multitude of issues that affect women's lives, such as poverty, illiteracy, and lack of reproductive freedom, among others. By framing these issues in the context of violence, we draw on the United Nations's recent recognition that acts of violence against women constitute human rights violations. Perhaps in raising these issues, clearer ways to link them to violence and to label them as kinds of violence in themselves may be found.

This could then be a means toward emphasizing the detrimental and often debilitating effects these issues have on women's lives. Where it is not feasible to argue that these human rights violations themselves are a form of violence, we might be able to contextualize violence as a catalyst in order to propel these other human rights abuses forward. The challenge is to allow violence to remain a central issue, while using its primacy in the public mind as a vehicle to bring forward less obvious, less tangible, less visually compelling or verbally emotive issues into the human rights framework.

Framing the Explanation: Gendered, Integrated Approaches

Inquiries that flow out of, and are influenced by, the decisions of who to invite to the table, and what the focus of the inquiry will be, involve searching for an explanation for what is happening, and the creation of a strategy to combat the problem. Do we isolate a gender element to highlight the unique manner in which women are being targeted and oppressed? Do we then call for separate, gender-based remedies - *i.e.*, the "outsider" approach? Do we instead use a gender lens to create epistemological frameworks which take into account other oppressions and build toward remedies that integrate gender as an essential factor, but not the sole factor, in redressing human rights abuses?

In answering these questions, we must consider how to examine the gender- based aspect of women's human rights without isolating it from the multiplicity of factors that influence it. How do we isolate women's common experiences of, and responses to, human rights abuses, from the vast array of differences that distinguish women from each other, *i.e.*, their perceptions, their perspectives, their goals? Where is the common ground that allows women to unite, yet frees them to assert their unique histories, cultures, and identities? How do we label these abuses "gender-based," while discussing the multiple factors that may have led to their existence or commission?

We struggle with these questions in order best to address the full range of women's realities, which, in fact, represent intertwined oppressions. At times, gender must be singled out as an important factor if only to compensate for the failure of the international human rights community to recognize the human rights of women after so many years. Yet, though separating the gender aspect may prove politically advantageous, we cannot allow women's lives to be compartmentalized, excluding some while privileging others in the process. The goal is to organize across boundaries, acknowledging similarities while simultaneously honoring differences, and to push for full recognition of the broad range of human rights violations women encounter in their lives. In the long run, this approach will be stronger because it is built on a foundation of genuine agreement (even if, at times, it is an agreement to disagree) and not of superficial unity.

In developing such an integrated approach, we must guard against the "add woman and stir" formulation. Repeated attempts to 'add women' to traditional categories and accounts expose the extent to which those accounts take male experiences as the norm. Insofar as 'adding women' means adding 'that which constitutes femininity,' it is impossible for women to be included in categories and theories whose definitions presume masculinity (*e.g.*, formal politics, public authority, economic power, freedom). In other words, women and conventional frameworks often cannot coexist.

Accordingly, "adding women" without altering existing frameworks for analysis requires women to force themselves into constraining, and often inaccurate categories, in order to make a connection between what is being described and their own realities and experiences. Often even a false, forced fusion is simply not possible. As Marysia Zalewski points out, in illustration of this dilemma: No amount of 'adding women' to the Social Contract theories of Hobbes and Locke could eradicate oppression if indeed the social contract is predicated on a 'Sexual Contract,' assigning women to be the property of men in civil (patriarchal) society.

Instead of simply adding women to existing epistemological frameworks, an integrated approach should seek to challenge current, traditional frameworks and attempt to create new, gendered ones, constructed to fit the way women, in all their diversity, view the world. Here, too, recent feminist work reflects this understanding. We must continue to pursue this course and not be swayed by the resistance to our demands by the institutions and structures blocking our progress.

Gendered frameworks for thinking about oppressions need not place women into an imaginary, unitary "woman's view." On the contrary, gendered frameworks can and should acknowledge explicitly that women view the world in diverse ways. Simultaneously, however, certain commonalities bind women's views together and permit the construction of frameworks out of the diversity. That commonality must be distilled, not only out of women's experiences of subordination, invisibility, and disempowerment, but out of their positive experiences and acts of self-empowerment as well. When the multiplicity of views among women is accounted for, and translated into a cohesive, holistic analysis, this diversity becomes "fundamentally different from mere competing perspectives inhabiting the world," instead, taking the form of a broad-based feminism. Though not all women are feminists, and many women do not see the problems they encounter as injustices resulting from their gender, feminist theories that are truly inclusive incorporate these differences as part of the diversity of women. While multiple ways of being feminist exist, a core of feminist thinking can encompass our differences while building on our similarities.

The best of feminist approaches "view gender as a fundamental ordering principle in today's world, value women's diverse ways of being and knowing, and promote the transformation of gender... hierarchies" and other power imbalances. Underlying the integrated approach, then, is an assumption that women reject power imbalances that render their lives subordinate and invisible.

Whenever such an approach relies on generalizations of women's experiences, it does not imply a common viewpoint among women nor posit homogeneity.... It does presuppose that patriarchal social relations have systematic social consequences and that mapping such consequences is valuable for corrective as well as constructive purposes.

An integrated approach toward women and human rights should, in the manner described above, continue to reject efforts by the formalized human rights structure to keep women isolated in a separate, segregated realm that too often minimizes their multiplicity, and continue to insist that social, cultural and economic human rights, so vital to the well-being, integrity and advancement of women, be treated on equal footing with civil and political rights. We must continue to call for the expansion of traditional "male" human rights categories while simultaneously emphasizing the intersectionality of all human rights. To do this, the framework itself must be expanded to incorporate a genuine analysis of the gender factor in all areas of human rights theory, development, and practice. An approach that recognizes the limitations of conventional epistemological frameworks need not simply be deconstructive. It may be reconstructive as well, designing new, gendered frameworks for thinking about the links between oppressions and the paths toward solutions. This approach cannot exist apart from women's multiple lived realities. It will only be meaningful if a broader range of "inside women" are brought to the table and heard.

CONCLUSION

Women's efforts in Vienna set the stage for the 1995 Beijing World Conference on the Status of Women and for much of the international work on women's human rights. As such, the fruit of these efforts provides fertile ground for expanding the women's human rights dialogue within the international framework and to be more inclusive of a broad array of diverse voices. The future work of women in the human rights arena should not be constrained by the limitations posed by the formal structure in Vienna and elsewhere. The Vienna Declaration, while a powerful document, should not be allowed to subvert feminist efforts to build a more expansive conception of human rights for women, and for all people.

Through this essay, we seek to demonstrate and emphasize why theorizing about, and, in particular, organizing for international women's human rights at every level, must include the leadership, contribution, input, and even domination of those women closest to the center of the insider perspective. In this context, we argue that an organizing strategy should be employed that, while raising gender-specific solutions, views them as short term and focuses on creating a gendered framework for thinking about oppressions and, where possible, through such framework, builds towards full integration of gender issues in the human rights dialogue, drawing connections between oppressions and communities without ranking or minimizing them but emphasizing their inter-relationships.

By suggesting an insider approach that encompasses the broadest range of voices possible, and in so doing raises the full spectrum of women's human rights concerns, and works toward broad, integrative measures to address them, we seek to continue the dialogue on ways to ensure these demands are inclusive and expansive yet viable in the mainstream human rights community.

2

Reflections on Emerging Frameworks of Health and Human Rights

Public health and human rights are "powerful, modern approaches to defining and advancing human well-being" and so are potentially powerful tools for generating change. Yet public health and human rights have also, at times, been powerful tools for maintaining the status quo, reinforcing hierarchies of power and domination based on race, gender, and class. Thus, just because a concern or policy or program adopts the label "health" or "human rights" does not give it unqualified value. To create a workable framework for health and human rights collaboration, we need first to define human well-being; only then will it be possible to clarify how the tools of public health and human rights can be used to advance that vision of it.

Perhaps because of this background and orientation, our view health and human rights advocacy as an essentially subversive activity, in the sense that my vision of "defining and advancing human well-being" ultimately requires overturning deeply-rooted social and political structures that produce ill health and that prevent all people-women and men from fulfilling their highest potential as human beings. But the goal is not to destroy: it is to transform and create. The structures that now obstruct human well-being must be changed into modes of social organization and interaction that will promote and support it. The disciplines of public health and human rights offer ways of thinking, of working, and of organizing that can ultimately give expression and concrete direction to that endeavor.

THE TOOLS OF PUBLIC HEALTH

Public health is a quintessentially social enterprise. Whereas medicine looks at the biological mechanisms of disease in individual people, public health looks at patterns of health and disease in populations. Most critical for present purposes, public health focuses on the links between an individual and the environment (physical, social, cultural, political, and/or economic) in which she lives, seeking in that linkage both an explanation for her health status and a potential entry point for policies and programs to address it.

The primary research and analytical tool of public health is epidemiology. Using statistics and probability theory, epidemiologists document a particular health phenomenon (e.g., maternal death) and measure the strength of its association with particular "risk factors" (e.g., maternal age or parity). Through this measurement, epidemiologists quantify risk; they measure the probability that a particular health phenomenon will occur if a particular risk factor is present. When a sufficient likelihood of an association is repeatedly found, the epidemiologist can state with reasonable confidence that the association is "real," i.e., it is not due to chance, bias, or poor study design. From such an association between a phenomenon and a risk factor, as well as additional information, the epidemiologist can infer-not prove-causality. That understanding of possible causal relationships can then form the basis for making effective public health policies and programs.

To many activists this may sound like a dry and tedious exercise, but in fact it has truly revolutionary potential. Nancy Krieger, in an insightful chapter about the politics of public health data, tells the story of how Louis René Villermé (1782-

1863), one of the founders of epidemiology, used his classic study of mortality in early 19th century Paris to challenge theories of disease causation that had prevailed in European medical thought for nearly 2000 years. In this study, Villermé first documented and ranked variations in mortality rates across different neighborhoods in Paris. He then attempted to correlate the variation in mortality with variations in environmental factors such as altitude, seasonal temperature, humidity, and quality of air, water, and soil, all of which were thought to cause disease. In this first ever systematic test of long-accepted environmental theories of disease causation, it turned out that none of these factors could account for the differences in mortality rates.

Looking for an alternative explanation, Villermé turned to the field of sociology, just then emerging in Europe, to develop hypotheses about the effects of social factors such as poverty and wealth on health. This time he calculated the proportion of households in each neighborhood that were exempt from rent tax, which was levied only on the wealthy, in order to arrive at a proxy measurement for poverty. He then correlated those proportions with the mortality data. The result was an "almost perfect fit": the neighborhoods with the lowest mortality also had the lowest proportion of tax-exempt households (i.e., were the wealthiest), while the neighborhoods with the highest mortality rates had the highest portion of tax-exempt households (i.e., were the poorest). Villermé thus concluded that social factors such as wealth and poverty (factors amenable to manipulation through public policy) were the principal causes of wide variations in mortality-a conclusion that, as Krieger pointedly notes, was not unrelated to the politics of his own time and place:

Villermé's ability to reach this conclusion in turn was shaped by the rapidly changing political realities and debates of his times: living in an era that saw the rise of industrial capitalism and the defeat of monarchies and mercantilism, Villerme, a firm supporter of the free market, could conceive of and receive public funds for investigating relationships between societally-produced-as opposed to divinely ordained-wealth, poverty, and disease. Villerme's study is a classic example of the basic methodology employed by epidemiologists; it also helps demonstrate several points that are key to this discussion about the potential for health and human rights collaboration. As Krieger points out, Villerme's important findings about the nature of disease "did not depend on technological or bio-medical breakthroughs, but upon broadening the 'natura' discourse of science with explicitly political concepts."

Moreover, what was (and is) uncritically accepted in science as "natural" and therefore immutable, has often served as effective camouflage for those in power to promote their own social and political goals-a phenomenon repeatedly uncovered in the histories of medical and "scientific" approaches to women's reproduction, to racial differences, and to colonial health policy. The influence of political ideology on health research and policymaking is fairly easy to see and accept in historical studies, especially with the benefit of nearly two centuries of hindsight, as in the example of Villerme. It is far more difficult to recognize and expose such assumptions when they are embedded in the daily discourse and routine work of public health today. To illustrate how politically or culturally conditioned assumptions about women's roles and lives influence current public health research and practice, I examine one chapter from the growing literature on the health effects of structural adjustment programs.

In an essay entitled "A Public Health Approach to the 'Food-Malnutrition-Economic Recession Complex,"' Leonardo Mata challenges the contention that shrinking food availability caused by economic crisis has led to declining child health. He questions whether economic conditions have significantly changed the "nutritional state and survival of children in less developed countries" because, in fact, the unavailability of food is not the usual cause of malnutrition and infant/child death. He demonstrates that infant and child mortality in developing countries is more often a complex interaction between malnutrition and infection conditioned by a multitude of factors other than the mere lack of food.

Mata then points to the fact that, given precisely the same financial resources and physical environment, certain children thrive while others are swept into the spiral of malnutrition and infection that ultimately ends in death or permanent disability. From this observation, Mata concludes that the true cause of poor child health is not lack of food: it is what Mata calls "deficient maternal technology." He defines "good" maternal technology as consisting of the following:

a. Adequate knowledge and technique for preparation and administration of weaning foods;
b. Appropriate handling of human and animal feces;
c. Knowledge about signs and symptoms of dehydration and other life-threatening conditions;
d. Acceptance of immunizations and other elements of modern medicine;
e. Basic nutrition and health education; and
f. Proclivity towards family planning.

Perhaps "technology" is the key word here, for Mata perceives a woman's inability to promote her children's health as primarily a failure to learn the technical lessons of primary health care. Nodding slightly to some vague social factors that may influence a woman's ability to protect her children, Mata tries to be careful not to lodge moral blame against mothers who fail. On the other hand, Mata stresses, faced with similar circumstances, some women seem to do just fine:

> Mothers are not entirely responsible for inadequacies in maternal technology, inasmuch as they are trapped in ecosystems and societies that have not permitted them to acquire an understanding and knowledge of the ubiquitous fecal contamination of food and environment and other threats to child nutrition and survival. On the other hand, many women in villages and slums possess effective maternal technologies, and their children thrive well despite the odds and hardships.

For Mata, the implications of his insight are clear: food programs to buffer the effects of economic crisis and structural adjustment are not the solution, because lack of food is not the problem. Rather, poor mothers are the problem; thus-improving maternal technology-creating better mothers-must be central to the solution.

Of course, Mata is not wrong when he states that a mother who makes sure the family's food is free from fecal contamination is more likely to have a healthy child than a mother who ignores the risks of contamination. Indeed, Mata and others who support his view probably would concede quite readily that in many cultures, the subordination of women does much to prevent them from learning or implementing the lessons of sanitation. The problem with the view exemplified by the Mata chapter is that it fails to invest that subordination of women with any importance, programmatically or theoretically.

By failing to pay attention to the elements of women's lives that lie outside the mother-child relationship-by failing to ask the right questions in his comparison of the children who thrive and those who die-he fails to see the multiple, fundamental ways in which economic crisis jolts women's lives and intensifies unequal gender and power dynamics within their households. These are dynamics that all too often lead to violence, marital breakdown, mental illness, and abject despair, and so, to an inability to cope with the effects of economic crisis. At the same time, the intense focus on the mother-child relationship, and the tendency to view women as isolated actors whose sole role in life is the birth and rearing of children, obscures the incredible strength, assertiveness, and resourcefulness that many women have shown in the face of crisis, developing and carrying out strategies that require them to go well beyond conventional gender roles of wife and mother in order to insure their own and their families' survival.

Thus, where Mata points to "maternal technology" as the solution to children dying from malnutrition-infection complex, other defensible solutions could be to change (or abandon) structural adjustment programs so that even children in families least able to cope with crisis can survive; and/or to facilitate women's ability to cope by taking measures to increase their autonomy, power, and rights within the families and communities devastated by adjustment programs. The public health practitioner trained only in the techniques of primary health care, and conditioned to think of them as "magic bullets" of unquestioned benefit, all too often will accept uncritically a conclusion such as Mata's. But the feminist or human rights activist attuned to the political implications of medical practice and health policy will likely ask a different set of questions to understand the dynamics of the household and communities in which children die during economic crisis. Such questions yield a different range of policy conclusions, possibly with primary health care (albeit wrapped in a different implementation package) among them.

Finally, there is another, more general observation to make about the approach exemplified in the Mata chapter.

Even when the potential influence of social factors such as macroeconomic crisis and structural adjustment programs is acknowledged, public health policymakers and practitioners often resort, almost reflexively, to the same kind of solution: individuals must modify their own behavior. In the case of women, this often means they must become "better" wives, mothers, or homemakers. This is a theme that has been repeated over and over again in current public health discourse and practice, particularly when it comes to health problems prevalent in marginalized populations.

For example, individual behavior change has long been the central theme in HIV/AIDS prevention policy, exhorting all people to "just say no" or to engage only in safer sex practices. Yet, for women who are powerless and vulnerable, caught in marital and sexual relationships over which they have little control, such advice may be worse than useless. Programs that address, or at least recognize, the power imbalances that shape women's lives, are now beginning to receive increased attention as the HIV/AIDS pandemic continues to ravage vast parts of the world. But in the United States, at least, this focus on individual behavior as the source of and solution to all social ills is now reaching new rhetorical heights with the Republicans' Contract with America and its cynically-titled centerpiece, "The Personal Responsibility Act" which purports to address the public health issues of "teenage pregnancy and illegitimacy" as well as the budget deficit, by penalizing indigent women who have children.

This discussion certainly does not mean to imply that individual behavior change is irrelevant to improving health and preventing disease. Indeed, I would argue that, as a matter of human rights, individuals must be empowered to make the kinds of decisions about their lives that will enable them to protect their health. But it is also critical to recognize that the decision to focus on individual behavior to the exclusion of other social determinants of ill health is a political choice; it is not an inescapable answer compelled by an indisputable, "scientifically correct" understanding of disease causation. Moreover, the model of behavior modification that typically underlies public health campaigns incorporates a kind of individualism associated with biomedical approaches to, health that actually does little to empower people to make such changes. As Elizabeth Fee and Nancy Krieger explained it in their chapter on the history of HIV/AIDS paradigms:

The biomedical model is also premised on the ideology of individualism. Adopting the notion of the abstract individual from liberal political and economic theory, it considers individuals "free" to "choose" health behaviors. It treats people as consumers who make free choices in the marketplace of products and behaviors, and it generally ignores the role of industry, agribusiness and government in structuring the array of risk factors that individuals are supposed to avoid. There is little place for understanding how behaviors are related to social conditions and constraints or how communities shape individuals' lives. This kind of abstract individualism will surface again in subsequent sections that consider the prevailing conceptions of rights which, like biomedicine, are influenced by liberal theory. But to summarize here: Public health tools and epidemiology in particular, expand our ability to see, to understand, indeed to measure, important aspects of the individual's relationship with the world. The fact that epidemiology is grounded in specific contexts, that it is based on statistical measurements that are testable and repeatable, is critically important to practice and effective advocacy. But we must beware of the "false conflation between scientific; objectivity and value-free science." Epidemiology-whether the question is which data to gather, how to interpret data we have, or how to craft policies and programs based on the data-will never be value-free, nor do I argue that it should be. But epidemiology and the tools of public health are just that-tools, and methodology. The values that drive their theory and practice cannot be found internally within epidemiology; they must come from outside of it.

Can health, then, be a value, a "good," in and of itself? My answer is emphatically yes. Only a person blessed with perfect health and blind to the suffering of others could have the arrogance to seriously propose otherwise. Hence, my point here is not to deny that health has biological dimensions or to belittle the importance of physical health as a worthwhile policy goal; rather, my point is to show that even an individual's physical health-not to mention her mental and emotional health-is inextricably tied to the wider conditions of her life. Thus physical health cannot be detached from political and social concerns, posited as an objective state of biological being, and then treated as though the choices we make in pursuit of it are apolitical and compelled by some internal logic that derives solely from health itself.

Yet, the influence of this detached and narrowly bounded view of health is so deep and pervasive in Western biomedical models and the social policies that derive from them, that its impact and operation can be extremely difficult to recognize and even harder to contest. Of course, the inability to perceive the influence of narrow health models or to grasp the fundamental truth that health is socially produced, is a malady that primarily afflicts those of us who are academics, theorists, policy analysts, or health professionals and have been born, bred, and/or trained in the ideology of science and Western biomedicine. By contrast, for the people in every part of the world, north and south, who live the reality of deprivation and discrimination in its harshest forms, the truth of the social production of health and disease is painfully obvious-even if its solutions are not.

Human rights are fundamentally about the struggle to make their voices heard and heeded. In a sense, then, the collaboration between health and human rights begins here, with the struggle to decide whose view of health will control the policies and programs that address it. Perhaps nowhere is this struggle more contentious, or the collaboration between health and human rights more urgent, than in the area of women's reproductive health and reproductive rights.

ALTERNATIVE VISIONS OF HEALTH AND RIGHTS

The reproductive health and reproductive rights movements grow from the conviction that at the core of human dignity lies the ability to be an effective agent in guiding the course of one's own life. Much of the work by activists and theorists in this field is devoted to understanding what exactly this means across different cultures and political systems and to finding the social structures and cultural configurations that will promote and support it. That work is underway, but far from complete.

The evolving understanding of reproductive health advocated by women's movements and many others in the public health field incorporates a broad, holistic, multi-faceted approach to women's health and health care; as theoretical understandings of reproductive health continue to develop, important initiatives on the ground can and do address specific health concerns in effective ways. There is certainly much to be said from a clinical or programmatic perspective about how such reproductive health initiatives are being designed and implemented (and, indeed, about how they contribute to the advancement of human rights, even if they are not ever perceived as human rights initiatives). But, for explanatory purposes here, it is a perhaps easier to describe what reproductive health and reproductive rights are by showing what they are not, or rather, by showing what these movements have reacted against.

In the health field, they have reacted against population control efforts that treat women as "targets" of contraceptive programs, blatantly manipulating their reproductive capacity in order to achieve demographic goals-goals set by dominant elites in pursuit of any number of different political agendas. They have reacted against maternal/child health policies that view the health of women as an instrument to ensure the health of children, and not as an important or valuable matter in its own right. They have reacted against medical institutions that focus on different pieces of women's bodies as discrete biological systems to be prodded, probed, and fixed, rather than seeing women's health as women live it, as part of complex interactive systems tied inextricably to the broader conditions of their lives. And they have reacted against domination by health professionals who present "risk" as if the only thing at stake in deciding whether or not to conceive or give birth is the possibility of physical injury; who obsess about reproduction but ignore sexuality; who preach about "personal responsibility" but fold on questions of power and resources, of vulnerability and discrimination.

This struggle around reproduction goes far beyond the health field, for women's reproduction is viewed as the primary tool for many other political projects as well. Thus, in many societies, a woman's sexuality and reproduction are symbols of her family's honor, to be guarded, watched, and controlled. They are the weapons with which the wars of identity politics are waged; most brutally, they are the scene of "ethnic cleansing." It is these political projects, and many others like them, against which the reproductive health and reproductive rights movements have been forced to define themselves.

Thus, stated in the negative, reproductive health and reproductive rights-indeed, human dignity-are about the right not to be alienated from one's own reproductive and sexual capacity; the right not to have that capacity used as an instrument to serve the interests of other individuals, collectivities, or states without one's consent and without the opportunity to participate in the political processes by which such interests are defined. Stated in the affirmative, the reproductive health and reproductive rights movements are about shifting perspectives, about changing whose point of view, whose values, whose experience, whose choices will control women's reproduction.

Such a shift in perspective will not happen automatically by force of logic, nor will it grow out of a movement that focuses on health alone, or on health as a biological problem to be addressed solely through improved medical techniques. It can only happen when health is understood as a function of the same forces that structure a woman's relationship to the physical and social world around her, and is addressed in policies, programs, and activist movements as such.

Once health is understood in this way, then improving health necessarily means dismantling the systems that have wrested away from women the ability and entitlement to decide the meanings and uses of their bodies and their lives. But it also means building social systems that promote and support women as effective actors who are vested, committed, inseparable and indispensable parts of the families, communities, and states within which they live. This second task, the task of renovating or rebuilding, is not an optional afterthought. It is the essence of the search for human dignity and social justice that is the basic motivation for human rights advocacy. But for that search to be successful, human rights will need to be reclaimed and reshaped to fit a movement that seeks to reflect the experiences and serve the visions of women in diverse cultural and political settings.

RECLAIMING HUMAN RIGHTS

If "health" as a political category has a problematic history for women's advocates, so too do "rights." Indeed, feminist theorists have been among the most articulate critics of rights-based legal regimes. While it is surely important for women's advocates and activists to consider these arguments, it is also essential to look beyond the academic debate surrounding rights; to acknowledge the different historically-grounded meanings that "rights" can have to the people who assert them; to assess the ways that rights language has been used and manipulated in international discourse; and then to make a strategic decision about the potential utility of health and human rights collaboration in advancing the ultimate goals of their work. This is an ongoing, dynamic process that will not yield one "correct" strategic answer, but rather, different answers at different times and places, all of which can effectively contribute to the same, shared political goals.

Moreover, it is an exceptionally complex inquiry because it involves not only sensitivity to political dynamics at the international level (e.g., in UN conferences, in bilateral or multilateral governmental relationships, and in the increasingly influential world of international NGOs) but also a sensitivity to the multitude of ways in which international developments interact with very diverse and specific local realities in every part of the world.

Of course, a full treatment of all these issues is again well beyond the scope of these preliminary reflections about health and human rights. In the section that follows, therefore, I attempt only to give a very broad-brush, almost impressionistic, sense of conventional approaches to human rights, women's responses to them, and the political use that various forces have found for both. In doing so, I focus most heavily-even if still only superficially-on a few key aspects of a much bigger set of problems and on one key area of concern (reproductive health and rights) in the hope of stimulating more critical attention to the broader challenges we face as the field of health and human rights develop.

A. Conventional Approaches and Feminist Critiques

Human rights are conventionally approached as a formal body of law codified in treaties, conventions and covenants. This law was first articulated in its contemporary form in the Universal Declaration of Human Rights (1948) and then further elaborated in legally binding instruments in the International Covenant on Civil and Political Rights (ICCPR) and the International Covenant on Economic, Social, and Cultural Rights (ICESCR) (1966), all of which together form what has sometimes been called the "International Bill of Rights." As an expression of basic values of human dignity and social justice, human rights draws inspiration from and resonates with historical and contemporary legal traditions of many different societies and cultures around the world. However, as a body of formal law dealing primarily with the relationship between individual citizens and their governments, human rights took its initial doctrinal inspiration from concepts of civil liberties found in Western legal systems which, in turn, derive largely from liberal political and economic theory.

That theory, in its classical formulations, embraces an ideology of individualism that has been the lightning rod for much of the criticism of rights. Closely associated with the theory and operation of a capitalist free market economic system, liberal individualism views people abstractly, as self-made, self-contained, separate individuals, isolated from others, pitted against the collective, pursuing their economic self-interest without reliance on the state. In a world so conceived, the purpose of rights is to stake out and protect a sphere of personal freedom; but that freedom is imagined as one built on boundaries: its essence is the right to keep others out, the right to be left alone.

In a legal system premised on such a world view, freedom from others also depends on enforcing the separation between the public and the private: rights are theoretically meant to keep the state out of the private sphere all together, and to operate most meaningfully in the public sphere where they regulate the individual's participation in public life and civil society, and his or her interaction with the law enforcement mechanisms of the state (police and court systems). Thus civil and political rights include such areas as freedom of speech and association, freedom from torture and from cruel, inhuman, or degrading treatment and punishment, the rights to a fair trial, and to life, liberty, and security of person (traditionally interpreted to refer to matters such as genocide, arbitrary arrest and detention, and execution). These civil and political rights, codified in the ICCPR, are often called "negative" rights because they are aimed at limiting the state's ability to encroach on individual freedom, at stopping the state from arbitrary or coercive actions.

By contrast, economic, social, and cultural rights, often called "positive" rights, deal with the state's obligation to create the affirmative conditions that help ensure human well-being. They include such matters as rights to health, education, employment, and housing. By ratifying the ICESCR, a State party "undertakes to take steps to the maximum of its available resources, with a view to achieving progressively the full realization of the rights recognized in the present Covenant by all appropriate means, including particularly the adoption of legislative measures." Although these positive rights were certainly central to the initial expansive conception of human rights embodied in the 1948 Universal Declaration, for a variety of reasons-some practical and some political-work in the human rights field has centered almost exclusively on the protection of civil and political rights. Most human rights NGOs have chosen not to address economic, social, and cultural rights, in part because of the near total absence of any methodology to monitor enforcement or define violations of them. Not surprisingly, governments have been equally reluctant to tread on this uncharted territory where implementation implies not just refraining from wrongful action, but also affirmative steps to alter the distribution and spending of public and private resources.

Failure to maintain the interconnection between positive and negative rights is among the primary criticisms that have been levelled against liberal theory and the rights-based legal systems it spawned. At the heart of these criticisms is a fundamental challenge to the notion that people exist as atomistic, disconnected, self-enclosed individuals. A legal system premised on a strict dichotomy between individuals and the collective ignores the extent to which individuals define themselves through, and take meaning from, their relationships with others; it fails to recognize the extent to which "we come into being in a social context that is literally constitutive of us."Seeing the individual primarily in opposition to the collective, liberalism supports the prevailing "negative" view of rights that is designed essentially to keep the state in check and as far out of social and economic life as possible. Within the international human rights scheme, this means emphasizing civil and political rights rather than economic, social, and cultural rights and maintaining a strict distinction between them. As women's human rights advocates have repeatedly pointed out, this distinction results in a formalistic and ultimately hollow view of rights.

For example, the right to decide on the number and spacing of children, however important to a women's health in theory, actually means little in a woman's life in fact, if there are no health services in place and no contraceptives available. More specifically, feminist critics of liberal, rights-based legal systems have demonstrated how conventional interpretations of such laws-including international human rights law-reflect the experience and interests of male elites and fail to accommodate or acknowledge the realities of women's lives. Their analyses elucidate the myriad ways in which the separation of the public and the private deflects the reach of rights from the site of women's most pervasive exploitation and deepest vulnerability-the domestic sphere-and obscures the crucial role that women play in the public sphere as we11.26 Though liberal legal systems purport to eschew all interference in the private sphere, particularly the family, feminist critics have shown that it is precisely the operation of such systems of law that structures the most intimate matters of private and family life, rendering the stated ideal of non-interference an incoherent principle and the purported neutrality of law an illusion.

B. The Political Context of Debates over Human Rights

At the international level, the debate over human rights has other, highly explosive, dimensions that take the discussion well beyond theory, into the harsh political reality within which women's movements operate internationally. Thus, any attempt to find a workable collaboration between health and human rights must also consider the ways that rights language has been manipulated for political ends that may have little to do with the defense or denial of the idea of rights *per se.*

In international discourse, the problem of rights is often posed as a series of oppositional dichotomies: universalism vs. cultural relativism; the individual vs. the collective; civil and political rights vs. economic, social, and cultural rights; North vs. South or East vs. West. The tensions that lie behind these dichotomies are real ones that need to be addressed carefully by the human rights community. I do not purport to do that here nor do I mean to dismiss such tensions lightly; rather, I wish to make a different point: while the tensions are real, the choice to *pose* the issues as either/or dichotomies presumes that the two poles exist only in opposition to each other and that the resolution can be only to choose one pole or the other. That is a presumption that serves particular political interests, as becomes clearer when we examine who is using these dichotomies and how they benefit from doing so; and when we see how structuring the problem this way becomes a tactic to be used against women internationally, in an effort to divide and silence us.

Perhaps a start in the bigger task of unpacking and analyzing these dichotomies is to recognize that lying at the crux of the problem is this: foes of women's rights typically characterize any expression by women of their entitlement to guide the course of their own lives as a rejection and denial of any and all ties or responsibility to others or to the collective. In their scenario, there is no such thing as a woman who seeks and gains control over the conditions of her existence yet chooses to live a life built around commitments and connections to others; given the chance-allowed to escape from the domination of patriarchal families and communities-it is presumed that women will abandon those families and communities altogether, in an ghastly display of selfish and hedonistic individualism. This basic conception of the "uncontrolled" woman as a dangerous and destructive force explains, in part, why human rights, with its apparent defense of the individual as against the collective, has become so explosive, particularly when applied to women's reproduction and sexuality, the area in which control over women is guarded most jealously. Lest this seem like a melodramatic overstatement of the position of those who oppose women's rights, consider some of the recent pronouncements of leaders of that opposition. For example, in 1992, urging voters to reject the proposed Equal Rights Amendment that would have explicitly prohibited discrimination on the basis of gender, Pat Robertson, leader of the increasingly powerful Christian Coalition in the United States, made this now infamous statement:

"The feminist agenda is not about equal rights for women. It is a socialist, anti-family political movement that encourages women to leave their husbands, kill their children, practice witchcraft and become lesbians."

His statements were echoed in more apocalyptic, even if somewhat less picturesque, terms by representatives of the Holy See who, in 1994, led a determined effort to derail the International Conference on Population and Development (ICPD) and to undermine its Programme of Action, a document that explicitly endorsed concepts of reproductive health and reproductive rights and acknowledged their link to human rights. Portraying the Cairo Conference as "basically about a type of libertine, individualistic life style" being imposed by the United States under the sway of "a pervasive feminist influence" that amounted to "cultural imperialism, " the Vatican made no bones about how serious it deemed the threat to be:

"Civilization is at stake. We would be foolish to see in the Cairo conference anything else." The Vatican found willing allies for its position in parts of the Muslim world. In statements condemning the conference, officials at Cairo's Al Azhar University, perhaps the most prestigious institution for Islamic scholarship in the world, challenged the Programme of Action reportedly because it "aims to defend sexual relations between members of the same sex or between different sexes outside legal marriage," "undermines parental authority" and "might encourage prostitution." Such statements helped touch off a wave of threats from Muslim extremists opposed both to the Conference and, perhaps more significantly, to the Egyptian government. Such opposition was broadcast over loudspeakers during sermons in neighborhood mosques:

"We reject this conference... It is a Zionist and imperialist assault against Islam. This is a policy imposed on Egypt by the United States." Others, speaking to the international press, took their campaign to a more chilling level. As one leader of a militant group based in Cairo is reported to have commented:

"Some brothers are preaching against this corrupt, immoral conference in the mosques. But others may decide to defend Islam by killing, and they would be willing to die in the process. If the West is afraid of blood, it should stay away from us. "It is thus a slippery slide between and among women's assertion of the right to control their reproductive lives; charges of destructive individualism; the spectre of cultural imperialism; and the evocation of North against South, East against West. Of course, as implied by the discussion of liberalism above, this is not a wholly frivolous position: human rights as classically formulated are Western in origin; and the kind of oppositional relationship between individual and collective that was projected by human rights theory, at least in its conventional formulations, does differ from that lived in most social and cultural arrangements, North and South. Moreover, governments clearly have been selective in the accusations of human rights violations made against one another, often having economic or other ideological interests as the primary consideration. And interactions involving human rights NGOs do sometimes suffer from the same arrogance and myopia that plagues all kinds of cross-cultural exchanges. These are issues in the human rights field that must be taken seriously and handled with honesty and circumspection.

Nevertheless, the structuring of the discussion as a set of oppositional dichotomies and, worse, the conflation of each dichotomous relationship with the others, is disastrous for women in both North and South. When any assertion of individual entitlement by women is automatically characterized as betrayal of the collective, when women are forced to choose between an assertion of themselves and assertion of their national, ethnic, or religious identity, then they have lost the first battle-the battle to set the terms of the debate. When this battle is lost then the result is silence: silence from those in the South who fear the accusation that they are "feminist" or "Western;" silence from those in the North who fear the accusation that they are "cultural imperialists."

The characterization of feminism or women's rebellion against patriarchal structures as simply an alien, Western import denies and attempts to suppress the leading role that women from Asia, Africa, and Latin America have played in defining the terms and setting the direction of women's human rights movements and reproductive health and rights movements in their own countries and on the international stage. Moreover, it makes invisible the long and rich histories of women's resistance as individuals or as organized movements in those countries and in relation to the diverse cultures within them. Finally, this conflation of dichotomies takes the genuine and appropriate circumspection of women in the North who are seriously concerned that their own voices and perspective have dominated some parts of the women's movement, and converts it from useful self-reflection and self-criticism into a paralyzing prescription for political correctness that prevents them from hearing and supporting those women in the South who are taking courageous stands to assert their own visions of human rights. At the same time, it prevents women in the South from building alliances with or supporting the struggles of women in the North by characterizing any attempt to make such alliances or connections, even on an ad hoc basis for specific purposes, as a breach of a different prescription of political correctness, one that views everyone located in the North as undifferentiated agents of imperialism and Western hegemony.

There is obviously much more work to be done to understand the historical and contemporary connections among all these phenomena; and to understand their political use in international discourse about human rights generally and women's human rights and reproductive rights in particular, and the strategic options for resisting them. That work is now urgent, as the politico-religious right will clearly remain a powerful force in international politics for a long time. But it is also important for women's health and rights advocates to remember that these are not the only forces threatened by the idea of women's control over their own reproductive and sexual lives. For many years, resistance to women-centered reproductive health and reproductive rights has also come from much quieter, even if more powerful, quarters. Perhaps the most influential of these are certain of the most conservative segments of the population "establishment" that has set the direction for many of the population policies that national governments have implemented over the last four decades often with the help of, or under pressure from, bilateral and multilateral aid agencies.

This part of the population establishment certainly operates from a very different political agenda than the politico religious right. It is therefore instructive to see the extent to which both camps have been driven by similar assumptions, particularly the belief that if women are allowed to escape the control of patriarchal families, communities, and states, they will abandon responsibility for and commitment to the collective. Although this belief rarely surfaces in a strident or even explicit way in the writing or work of population and family planning specialists, its influence can be teased out nevertheless. For example, Susan Cotts Watkins, in a chapter entitled, "If All We Knew About Women Was What We Read in *Demography*, What Would We Know?" examines 25 years of this leading academic journal to try to understand the views of women that have driven demographers' work. She shows that demography as a field tends to share the basic view of liberal theory in which women are conceptualized as "separate selves," as "autonomous and impervious to social influence," and ultimately concludes that:

If all we knew about women was what we read in the chapters on fertility, marriage, and the family, we would conclude that women are primarily producers of children and of child services; that they produce with little assistance from men; that they are socially isolated from relatives and friends; and that their commitment to the production of children and child services is expected to be rather fragile (emphasis added).This description of demographers' view of women is startlingly contrary to many women's own views of themselves, to their feelings of commitment, their experience of connectedness, and their valuing of relationships (including relationships with their own and others' children, relatives, and friends)- as expressed in narratives, demonstrated in everyday life, and even proven in social science research.

Yet, in many parts of the world, population and health policies have been routinely built not around women's own experience of the world (as advocated by the reproductive health and reproductive rights movements), but around the assumptions and world view exposed by Watkins. The result is precisely the kinds of programs that evidence a deep distrust of women and the decisions it is presumed they would, make if given the chance. Thus, population policies and family planning; programs often tend to exclude women from planning and decision-making processes, and instead impose on them, through methods involving varying degrees of persuasion or coercion, the so-called professional's view of what is good for society, for families, for health and for women-and have the power of the state to back them up.

Given this orientation of the population establishment, it is important to recognize-and question why-they have historically been among the strongest advocates of recognizing "the right to decide freely and responsibly on the number and spacing of children" as a human right. Elsewhere, I have shown that when this was first articulated as a human right, at the 1968 Teheran Conference on Human Rights, a primary motivation was to find a wedge to get contraceptives into the many countries (especially in the South) where they were then illegal or otherwise blocked, in order to control population growth.

Although those within the population movement who advocated this human right no doubt genuinely believed that individuals should have the right to use contraceptives and to control their fertility, they perceived-the limits on an individual's right to decide whether to have children very differently from the way women's movements understood the same right when they promoted it.

In short, the primary goal of the population movement was to lower population growth, not to ensure that women themselves had both the right and the ability to control their bodies and lives; thus the "freedom" of the individual to decide was, in the view of the population movement, readily limited by the "responsibility" to make the fertility-limiting decision imposed by government population policies purportedly in furtherance of the greater good. As Susan Watkins put it, commenting on the special issue of Demography on family planning that was published in 1968, the year of the Teheran Conference, "Even when the language seems to empower women by claiming they have the right and the power to choose to control their fertility, they are expected to use this power to control world population growth."Apparently, then, the population control movement believed that in the human rights framework as conventionally understood, it had found a useful tool for advancing towards its own view of human well-being. Thus, one lesson is clear: human rights, like public health, can be wielded as a tool to promote quite particular political goals that might be substantially different from-even contrary to-the goals of women's advocates. This takes us back to the point made at the very start: while public health and human rights can be powerful tools for generating change, they can also be powerful tools for maintaining hierarchies of power and domination based on gender, race, and class.

Why Bother with Human Rights?

If rights, in their conventional interpretations, have failed to recognize or redress women's experience of violation; and if the human rights paradigm, when manipulated either by those who purport to accept it or by those who vehemently reject it, provides fodder to precisely the forces that seek to oppress women, then one might legitimately ask, why bother to use human rights at all? Aren't they more trouble than they are worth, particularly given the notoriously weak enforcement mechanisms in the international system?

My answer begins with the refusal to accept the dichotomies routinely imposed on the discussion. Human rights are strategically valuable because they express, in the broadest terms, basic values-human dignity and social justice-that have historical and contemporary roots in cultures throughout the world. But those values do not dictate a particular lifestyle, or identity, or way of being in the world. Rather, they affirm the fundamental value of human agency: the nature of human beings as effective, social actors.

When read carefully and interpreted in its fullest dimensions, the human rights paradigm enables us to reject as inaccurate and destructive the abstract individualism of liberal theory, the notion of individuals operating in isolation and crude self-interest, seeking to keep others at bay, even while imposing their will on everything, animate and inanimate, around them. At the same time, the human rights paradigm rejects treatment of any person as property, chained to another's or a group's will, to be dominated, controlled, and used. Rather, it seeks to create a world in which human dignity adheres in the still distant ideal of choice: the notion;

that human beings, constituted through relations with others, can still make choices about their lives, can still have something to say about how to structure and maintain relations with others, be they family, community, or state.

Such an ideal has particular power and importance in our time. In a world increasingly consumed by the most brutal struggles of "identity politics," a politics in which access to power and resources is sought to be determined by group identification, and group identification is prescribed by allegedly immutable characteristics of birth (e.g., race, ethnicity, even religion), then women-whose appearance, behavior and, particularly, sexual conduct, are made to be the symbols of "purity," the quality that is believed to ensure group strength and continuity-are most vulnerable to control and domination. At the same time, our world is increasingly, and irrevocably, international: in economics, politics, and communications, we are all now bound to each other through complicated webs of dependence, infiltration and, most painfully, inequality and domination. In such a world, human rights affirms the basic entitlement of all people to resources and to the respect and dignity that comes from the ability to consciously, willfully participate in setting the terms of their interactions with the world around them.

No one fools themselves into believing that we are close to such an ideal. No one fools themselves into thinking that its attainment will be easy or that it will come without massive social change, in which some will be required to relinquish power over others. But in the area of health, in which we can see in the most obvious physical terms the results of structures of inequality large and small, we have perhaps the best chance to make a difference, to determine and implement social configurations that can support and promote human well-being. In short, when human rights principles are applied to health, we begin to have the strategic, political basis upon which to mobilize across the divides of nation, culture, class, race, and religion, in support of each other and in pursuit of change.

RETHINKING THE CONNECTIONS BETWEEN HEALTH AND HUMAN RIGHTS

To use health and human rights collaboration in this way means rebuilding our understandings of both health and human rights, as well as the vision of human well-being they define and advance, from the ground up. It means taking full account of the very real differences that shape our lives, while giving full respect to our common humanity. It means approaching health and human rights collaboration not as a theoretical puzzle that is worked through in a political vacuum, but rather as a very concrete, contextualized inquiry that begins from the experience of those whose health and human rights are most at stake.

Such work will require the combination of many different approaches at the same time. For example, the women's human rights movement has effectively used the analytically simple, but emotionally and rhetorically powerful, method of personal testimony to force recognition of women's violation, entitlement, and need. This has happened most notably in the area of violence against women, where substantial progress has been made in changing perceptions in both the human rights field and the international health field. To a significant extent, such progress has come as a result of women's demand, quite simply, to be heard. In "tribunals" held in all parts of the world and also in international fora, women's often courageous testimonies of violence inflicted with impunity in both the private and public spheres, demonstrated more powerfully than any amount of academic analysis ever could, that both fields, locked into formalistic, narrow ways of understanding both rights and health, had failed to listen to or acknowledge the impact or importance of such experiences and so had effectively excluded this aspect of women's lives from their purview.

In the area of reproduction and sexuality, enormously valuable work that will ultimately contribute to new understandings of health and human rights, is being done in multidisciplinary, action-oriented field research. This includes, for example, the project being conducted by the International Reproductive Rights Research Action Group (IRRRAG) in seven countries in Africa, Asia, Latin America, and North America, to uncover and document the ways that women themselves understand and express their entitlement in matters of reproduction and sexuality; and the project conducted jointly by Health Action Information Network in the Philippines and the Institute for Development Research in the Netherlands, which through participatory action-research in multiple countries, focuses more specifically on women's experiences of fertility-regulating methods and reproductive health care. Such reconceptualizing of health and rights beginning with the experiences of women, will also require working at a more theoretical level to transform the way the very words we use in health and human rights work, are interpreted and understood.

For example, Rosalind Petchesky, in an essay entitled "Body As Property: A Feminist Re-Vision," attempts to "recuperate the notion of self-propriety"-the idea of "owning" or controlling one's body-by looking "at the variety of local meanings that women in non capitalist societies, radical democrats, and slaves have given to the idea of owning their bodies, as well as the value that contemporary feminists of color are placing on r-owning their bodies as an aspect of self-definition." As she puts it, "The `objects of property' may have more to tell us from their vantage point than we can learn from positioning ourselves within the debates of the treatises, the law books, and the political-theory canon."

As with women's approach to human rights more generally, Petchesky's point is not to make women's lives and claims fit within the four corners of the law as it currently is interpreted; rather, her point is to see how the powerful language so basic to that law-in this case, the concept of "property"-can be reshaped to serve the political goals defined by women. The aim is to understand "the language of self/body ownership as a rhetorical strategy for political mobilization and defining identities, not a description of the world." From this perspective, the very notion of "property" is given new meaning:

Rhetorical claims on behalf of women's ownership of their bodies invoke meanings of ownership as a relationship of right, use, and caretaking - meanings that have different cultural moorings from the commercial idea of property that the regime of triumphal international capitalism conventionally takes for granted.

The project she envisions has distinctly political importance:

Perhaps there are good reasons to defend this language particularly as it pertains to people's relationship to their bodies. Perhaps owning one's body is a necessary element of citizenship in an affirmative but noninterventionist state. All of these projects that focus intensely on the meanings that women in a wide range of different political, social, and cultural settings express for themselves, are vitally important for the ultimate collaboration between health and human rights. But if we are really to escape the abstract individualism of liberal theory and the biases it has imposed onto biomedicine and conventional rights interpretations-that is, if we are to demand that rights be understood not primarily as a right to build boundaries or to be left alone, but rather as a right to live with dignity in the context of social commitments and relationships-and if we are to demand that health and disease be understood not simply as a function of "free" individual behavioral choices, but rather as a result of lives constrained by social forces such as poverty and discrimination, then we will also need to develop a much more structural critique than can be gleaned from case studies or narratives or anecdotal evidence alone.

This is where public health and its tools hold great potential in strategic collaboration with human rights. As discussed much earlier, public health seeks to understand health and disease not simply as a function of self-contained biological systems of the human body, but also as a function of the wider conditions of a person's life. By looking not just at the health of the individual, but at patterns of health in populations, public health allows us to go beyond isolated anecdotes or incidents and to see social patterns and configurations associated with what is experienced as individual phenomena of death, disability, or disease.

An excellent example of this is a recent chapter by Susan Greenhalgh and Jiali Li that explicitly attempts to demonstrate how feminists can use the discipline and methodology of demography to reveal patterns and practices not observable through qualitative research. Working with data from a rural area of China, they show how the one-child policy has in practice, been shaped over time through "politics of resistance," then "negotiation," then "submission." By projecting to the population level and documenting the shocking shifts in sex ratios in different age and birth-order cohorts, they enable us to see more than simply a rash of cases of selective abortion or infanticide; rather, they can demonstrate how a policy that began as gender-neutral, ultimately has come to involve massive violence and discrimination against the youngest girls in China and, in the most profound ways, has inflicted terrible damage on the wider society as well. Arguing for the importance of developing a feminist demography, they point out

> It may be that the more politicized the arena of reproduction, the more crucial demographic evidence becomes, for where reproduction is heavily contested, people work hard to hide their secrets, not only from other members of their society but from social scientists as well. In China the discrimination and violence directed against little girls were thickly cloaked until large-scale demographic evidence brought them to light.

Not only do public health tools (including epidemiology and demography) help us identify and describe health issues as socially constructed human rights issues, they also begin to tell us what to do about them. This is critical in the area of positive rights, where the objective is not just to get the state to stop committing a violation, but rather to get the state to do the right thing to improve the social condition in question. Thus, epidemiologic evidence can show us not only the extent of a health problem and its general association with social conditions, it can also show us in far more refined ways, how particular social conditions interact with biological factors to yield patterns of ill health. It thus can help us determine where to begin to address state responsibility for dealing with a particular health issue.

But, as the earlier discussion of "deficient maternal technology" in the context of structural adjustment programs demonstrated, this is not a value-free exercise. When health data are analyzed from a feminist perspective (such as demonstrated in the Greenhalgh and Li chapter), essentially bringing a politicized view of human well-being to the endeavor, then the understandings developed from health research can begin to acquire the dimensions necessary to organize and advocate effectively within the framework of human rights law. Rather than simply shouting that something must be done to meet, for example, obligations to ensure a right to health under the ICESCR, we can begin to show that "progressive achievement of rights," requires very specific steps, and then demand that such steps be taken. Finally, it is important to see that health research can also be used the other way around.

Not only can we study particular health phenomena to understand how they are socially produced and can be socially ameliorated; we can also study particular human rights phenomena to understand their implications for health. Mann et al point out that a "coherent vocabulary and framework to characterize dignity and different forms of dignity violations are lacking," and suggest that "a taxonomy and epidemiology of violations of dignity may uncover an enormous field of previously suspected, yet thus far unnamed and therefore undocumented, damage to physical, mental, and social well-being." While this is certainly true, from the perspective of the affirmative building of health and human rights collaboration, we also need to study advancements in human rights. For example, while some feminist theorists are working from within legal and social science frameworks to "reconceive" the concept of autonomy (in somewhat the same way that Petchesky is doing with "property")," demographers and public health researchers are attempting to understand how changes in women's status/power/autonomy (variously defined) in many different social and cultural settings affect the health and well-being of women, their children and families, and their wider communities.

It is perhaps this research, as much as anything else, that actually built the momentum for the major shifts in perspective within the population and family planning community that were ultimately incorporated in the Cairo Programme of Action. Many years of careful public health research and writing provided the fuel for advocates of reproductive health and reproductive rights to elaborate and assert a women-centered approach. In the end, the proof that the well-being of all people-men, women, and children-depends on dramatic changes in the ability of women to set the course of their lives, became undeniable.

To a significant extent, that understanding is now incorporated in the theoretical literature and rhetorical statements that shape the population/family planning/maternal-child health fields-and thus the evolving reproductive health field is beginning, slowly, to convert them, in substantial part, in the reproductive health field. But it will take a human rights movement, one that insists on our common humanity yet respects our diversity, to give those statements real meaning in transforming the relationships of power that shape the health and lives of us all.

3

Culture and Cross-Cultural Dialogue

INTRODUCTION

This page considers whether international human-rights norms can provide a basis for legitimately criticizing traditional cultural practices and, if so, how such criticism might be appropriately structured. Clearly, this question is premised on a range of assumptions. The first assumption is that international human-rights norms apply to the conduct of non-state actors, a question not yet fully resolved. The second is that certain traditional cultural practices violate one or more international human-rights norms. Although contentions of this nature are frequently presented as self-evident, and suggest that we may profit from a closer analysis of these claims. At the very least, we should notice that they rest on judgements about the content of human-rights norms and whether particular cultural practices violate those norms.

If we accept that such judgements will be based on values that are culturally and historically bound, then it should come as no surprise that interpretative disagreement exists between, and perhaps within, different groups regarding these matters. The question for this chapter is how this dissent might be harnessed in a positive way in order to expand cross-cultural understandings of human rights and, if necessary, to legitimate criticisms of cultural practices within a human-rights framework. It is suggested that cross-cultural dialogue may be one way of achieving this purpose.

MEANING OF CULTURE AND CROSS-CULTURAL DIALOGUE

Although an exhaustive definition of "culture" is difficult to articulate, A.A. An-Na'im offers the following analysis:

Culture is the source of the individual and communal world view: it provides both the individual and the community with the values and interests to be pursued in life, as well as the legitimate means for pursuing them. It stipulates the norms and values that contribute to people's perception of their self-interest and the goals and methods of individual and collective struggles for power within a society and between societies.

It has been suggested that "cultures are dynamic and changing, both internally and in response to external forces and influences." It has also been suggested that this dynamism is an inherent part of the way cultures or traditions are determined. According to this view, traditions define themselves and are defined through two kinds of debate or dialogue: first, "internal, interpretative debates through which the meaning and rationale" of the tradition is expressed; and secondly, debates with those critics external to the tradition. In this sense, the very existence of "traditions" is contingent on some measure of cross-cultural dialogue.

The sense to use the term "cross-cultural dialogue" draws upon this inter-normative potential. In the human-rights arena, this means enhancing the cross-cultural legitimacy of human-rights norms through an appropriately framed cross-cultural dialogue, which both informs and is informed by internal re-interpretation of human-rights norms. In other words, the inevitable processes of cultural change and the evolution of cultural norms may be facilitated by cross-cultural dialogue. This approach recognizes that external criticism occupies an important role in the process of cultural change. At the same time, it avoids the formulation and expression of judgement or criticism reached by "evaluating one cultural construct with the categories of another". Rather, cross-cultural dialogue should be aimed at broadening and deepening international (or rather intercultural) consensus. This direction may include support for the proponents of enlightened perceptions and interpretations within a culture. This effort, however, must be sensitive to the internal nature of the struggle, endeavouring to emphasize internal values and norms rather than external ones.

In this sense, cross-cultural dialogue necessitates a certain level of self-awareness and introspection. This is critical for several reasons. First, it facilitates an awareness that the "formulation of the problem is already culturally bound". This awareness, in turn, encourages us to observe and criticize a particular human problem with the "tools of understanding" of the other culture, a process that requires an appreciation of the content and tenor of internal debates, in addition to the debate with outsiders. It may also contribute to our understanding of how relationships of dominance shape discourse within and between groups, both inside and outside the culture. It is critical to identify these hierarchies in order to determine whether the claims and ideologies expressed by particular groups reflect true consensus rather than assertions of internal power.

Most importantly, cross-cultural dialogue is-as the term "dialogue" suggests-a two-way process. This means that we must be prepared to submit our own cultural systems and practices to similar scrutiny by those outside our cultural context.

One hopes that by confronting the reality of cultural difference, rather than subsuming it under dubious claims to universality, human-rights norms might achieve greater cross-cultural legitimacy. At the very least, this approach should promote a foundation of understanding from which justifiable comment and criticism can be made, as opposed to criticism that is perceived as ignorant and disrespectful and which consequently impedes dialogue.

FEMALE GENITAL OPERATIONS AND THE MANY FACES OF CULTURE

This Part will critique the manner in which culture has been used by two groups: first, it will address those who argue that female genital operations are a cultural tradition that cannot be legitimately challenged; and secondly, it will respond to outsiders who argue that "culture" is merely invoked as a defence to mask a practice that is a manifestation of patriarchal oppression.

A. Culture as a Justification for Female Genital Operations

Although several forms of female genital operations have been documented, commentators generally identify three types, which are differentiated according to the quantity of tissue removed. There are, however, obvious difficulties with generalizing about the nature, scope and reasons for the practices since they exist in a wide variety of geographic, cultural, religious and socio-economic contexts. Many reasons overlap, and different communities may emphasize different explanations, or combinations of them, including the protection of women's chastity and honour, religious obligation, beliefs about female genitalia and fertility and tradition.

According to Slack, "the most widely held justification for the continuation of the practice is the need to maintain tradition." In some communities, genital operations constitute a rite of passage through which initiates are taught the lessons of "tribal unity and their specific position in maintaining tribal cohesion." On this basis, it has been argued that the practice is of great importance to both the individuals and the continued survival of the group. It permits individuals to identify with their heritage and to enjoy recognition as full social members of the group. In a similar vein, female initiation rituals have been credited with establishing strong networks of lifelong friendship, support and reciprocal obligation between women initiated together.

Some commentators have argued that in many societies, essential aspects of human dignity are ensured through membership in the community, rather than through inherent rights that attach to the individual. This approach forms the basis of the argument that international human-rights norms are based on a social organization derived from liberal philosophy, which does not accommodate unique African perspectives:

> Within the organisation of African social life one can discern various organising principles. As a people, Africans emphasise groupness, sameness, and commonality. Rather than survival of the fittest and control over nature, the African worldview is tempered with the general guiding principle of the survival of the entire community and a sense of co-operation, interdependence, and collective responsibility.

This perspective suggests that international human-rights standards, as presently articulated, are only one way (the Western way) of protecting human dignity. It is argued that the communitarian ideal to which African cultures adhere emphasizes the fulfilment of one's role in the community as a means of attaining one's identity. Accordingly, group considerations may have greater cultural legitimacy than individual rights. The irua initiation ceremony of the Gikuyu tribe has been used to illustrate this point:

> The main purpose of the irua ceremony is to persuade the initiates that they must give up their duty-free childhood individuality and become members of the community, where collective needs come first. Once an initiate becomes an adult member of the tribe, any conflict between the individual's own and family needs and the community's needs should be reconciled for the general good of society.

This being so, it might be argued that outsiders' condemnations of the practices not only fail to appreciate their cultural and communal significance, but are tantamount to imposing external cultural values on practicing cultures.

> The overwhelming majority of [Gikuyu] believe that it is the secret aim of those who attack this centuries-old custom to disintegrate their social order and thereby hasten their

Europeanisation. The abolition of irua will destroy the tribal symbol which identifies the age-groups, and prevent the Gikuyu from perpetuating that spirit of collectivism and national solidarity which they have been able to maintain since time immemorial.

Even those who do not support the practices in light of changing social and economic conditions caution against condemnation from outsiders.

Female mutilation is subjects that is taboo... But let us not rush into the error of condemning [genital mutilations] as uncivilized and sanguinary practices. One must beware of describing what is merely an aspect of difference in culture as barbarous. In traditional Africa, sexual mutilations evolved out of a coherent system, with its own values, beliefs, cultural and ritual conduct. They were a necessary ordeal in life because they completed the process of incorporating the child in society.

B. Rejection of Culture as a Basis for Female Genital Operations

While evidence exists to support the view that female genital operations enjoy wide community acceptance in practicing cultures, the relativist position presented above has been questioned extensively. First, African culture has been influenced significantly by colonialism and modernization. According to Howard, this has fundamentally changed the nature of relationships both within communities and between individuals and the state. Paradoxically, the process of modernization in the public sphere may have actually intensified the importance attached to those traditional practices that occupy the private sphere. A. Funder suggests: "In the face of rapid industrialization, global interdependence, and the modernization they bring, many countries cling to traditional practices as living symbols of the autonomy and continuity of their culture." Moreover, the most frequent arguments made in order to preserve culture mandate a strict separation between an increasingly global, high technology free marketplace, which is the public sphere of almost all countries, and a private sphere in which traditions and cultural practices may continue.

Indeed, Dorkenoo and Elworthy suggest that female genital operations continue to occur notwithstanding that today in many of these societies the ceremonial has fallen away; both excision and infibulation are performed at a much younger age that cannot be construed as having anything to do with entry into adulthood or marriage, and the child's role in society does not change at all after the mutilation.

Some feminist human-rights scholars advocate a cautious acceptance of the claim that female genital operations are a legitimate expression of cultural values. It has been argued that such claims are generally favourable to the powerful members within groups and, consequently, tend to mask the role of gender in shaping the interests, ideologies and practices of the group. Put simply, these claims may be expressions of internal power, used as a subterfuge for reinforcing oppressive gender roles. In an impassioned articulation of this position, F.P. Hosken states:

> This report makes it clear that these operations are more than sexual assault, more than physical torture and abuse. They represent a deliberate means to enslave women and a systematic attempt by men to subjugate women absolutely and life-long to physically control women's bodies, reproduction and sexuality.

On these bases, it has been argued that the continuation of female genital operations is as concerned with providing the means for a male-dominated power elite to control women's sexuality as it is with preserving cultural identity and cohesion. This argument rests on the assertion that female genital operations engender subordination by ensuring "female virginity before marriage, female fidelity throughout marriage, and heterosexuality". In this way, it has been argued that female genital operations serve the purpose of forcing women to submit to males and accept their socially prescribed gender roles. Through traumatic experiences of painful operations, childbirth and intercourse, women learn to submit to the males of their families and accept their secondary positions.

The patriarchal social organization and attendant social norms of some practicing communities may lend support to these analyses. Dorkenoo, for instance, observes that matrilineal African societies do not practise female genital operations, unlike many of their patrilineal counterparts. In a 1975 study of ethnically diverse infibulation- practicing communities in North-Eastern Africa, Hayes concluded that despite differences in economic and political organization, the traditional organizing principles of each group were patrilineal, patrilocal and patriarchal. Van der Kwaak observes that genital operations can also assume economic significance, particularly in communities where the bride-price is only paid to the father of a gabar gudban ("closed woman"). Referring to Hayes's work, Van der Kwaak surmises:

He practice is so resistant because of its important role for the continuity of the patrilinear kinship structure, articulated in a system of proclamations and prohibitions inserted in marriage practices, modesty code, family honour, women's social roles etc.

In these and similar circumstances, it is argued that women internalize the norms of their cultural milieu and, in turn, accept the practice because the ramifications of breaking with tradition can be severe. Uncircumcised women may bring disgrace on their families, are considered unmarriageable and promiscuous and risk ostracism from their group. Former Kenyan President Jomo Kenyatta, for example, insisted that female genital operations were crucial to the viability of Kenyan society and stated that "no proper Gikuyu would dream of marrying a girl who has not been circumcised, and vice versa".

C. Rethinking the Gender/Culture Dichotomy

The analyses that reject cultural explanations for female genital operations, while offering a useful critique of those arguments that favour preserving the custom, are weakened by the absence of substantial input from those women and men who may be engaged, and struggling for recognition, in the internal discourse on the subject. Without this input, outsiders are not only unable to support and influence the processes of internal discourse, but are incapable of accurately identifying and understanding the critical internal processes at work. This ostensibly allows outsiders to dictate the terms of the debate, an ultimately counter-productive situation, which can provoke allegations of imposing extra-cultural values and norms.

Western efforts to eliminate the practice, on the part of missionaries or colonial administrators, have simply served to confirm in people's minds that colonial destruction of traditional customs weakens their societies and exposes them to the ill-effects of Western influence.

This result is also reflected in the accusations of essentialism and cultural imperialism which have been levelled at Western feminist commentators.

Whatever the good intentions of Western feminists in expressing solidarity or "helping their sisters of color", Western articulations of concern over the contemporary practice of genital surgery in Third World nations are often perceived as only thinly disguised expressions of racial and cultural superiority and imperialism.

Western responses to this kind of criticism, however, have not always been positive:

> Critics from Western countries are constantly being intimidated by accusations of "racism", to the point of misnaming, non- naming, and not seeing these sado-rituals. The accusations of "racism" may come from ignorance, but they serve only the interests of males, not of women.

In the same way that the relativist view can be criticized for glossing over the importance of gender, some feminist analyses can be criticized for failing to adequately appreciate the importance of culture in defining women's experiences and priorities. Accordingly, these analyses are deficient in three important ways. First, they fail to convincingly explain why some women vehemently defend and perpetuate the practice. Secondly, by defining the issue exclusively along gender lines, these theories seem to overlook the potentially critical connections between adherence to tradition, colonialism and nationalism. Thirdly, they seem to presume that it is possible (or desirable) to universalize the female experience, thus, obviating the need for considering the specific perceptions, experiences and agendas of women in practicing cultures. This tends to deny those women the opportunity to articulate their experiences and priorities. Moreover, it denies that women are "agents of knowledge" and ignores the force of the internal debates and struggles in which these women may be engaged.

CENTRING AFRICAN WOMEN THROUGH CROSS-CULTURAL DIALOGUE

The purpose of this section is to extend the insights offered by relativist and feminist commentators by applying the principles of cross-cultural dialogue and proceed by adopting the following methodological approach: first, respecting differences between the cultural and historical contexts of those participating in the dialogue; secondly, recognizing the patterns of domination that exist (or have existed) between the cultures of respective participants, in addition to identifying the patterns of dominance that shape discussions within cultures; and, finally, engaging women from practicing cultures in the dialogue in an effort to discern an accurate picture of the struggles, priorities, concerns and hopes of those who may have been less prominent in the discussion. This approach is particularly important for outsiders who have concerns about the custom and who wish to assist women within practicing cultures because, as An-Na'im points out:

Heir claiming to know what is the valid view of the culture of that society will not accomplish this effectively. Such a claim would not help the groups the outsiders wish to support because it portrays them as agents of an alien culture, thereby frustrating their efforts to attain legitimacy for their view of the values and norms of their society.

A. Understanding Cultural and Historical Contexts

The idea that cultural and historical contexts are specific and extremely influential in structuring dialogue challenges us to be somewhat introspective. At the very least, participants in the dialogue need to consider how the social meanings attached to concepts like "individual", "group" and "harmful practices" are constructed within particular cultural and historical contexts. This, for instance, may require an appreciation of the different perspectives that liberal and communitarian philosophies bring to bear on particular issues like female genital operations. For example, many Westerners have responded to the practices with a sense of "moral outrage", perceiving the custom as a brutal violation of an individual's rights by the group. This, however, is not necessarily the response of women and men within practicing communities. In 1983, Asma El Dareer interviewed over 4,500 adults in Sudan to gauge their responses to female genital operations. Dareer found that 82.6 percent of women and 87.7 percent of men interviewed approved of female genital operations regardless of type (that is, sunna, intermediate or pharaonic). More recent studies indicate that approval rates among Sudanese women have declined, although they remain significant. A 1989-1990 Demographic and Health Survey found that seventy-nine percent of the respondents supported continuation of the practice, although strong opposition was recorded among urban women and women with secondary level education.

By contrast, "moral outrage" does not always accompany Western perceptions of "self-imposed" health problems facing women, such as self- starvation practices. As Gunning points out, however, the idea of women starving themselves for cosmetic purposes in societies where food is often scarce might be considered "morally outrageous". The relevant point is that because culture is a primary source of normative systems, it inevitably influences the processes of moral reasoning and perception.

Female genital operations and self-starvation have been the subject of comparison because in each case women participate in practices that may be harmful to them in response to broader social pressures (for instance, to emulate socially constructed ideals of beauty or womanhood). It might be argued that such a comparison is invalid because the community actually mandates the relevant practice in the former case, but it does not in the latter.

In other words, female genital operations are accorded community acceptance and are mandatory in many circumstances (a group-imposed practice), whereas self-starvation is generally acknowledged as a "problem" and is considered to result from aberrant individual behaviour (a self-imposed practice). Could it be, however, that the participatory role of the community is simply less direct, and therefore less visible, in the latter case? Does the Western cultural emphasis on "individual freedom" (and therefore individual responsibility) obscure the role of the community in contributing to the problematic behaviour? Even if Westerners see self-starvation as a problem which requires redress, there may be less general support for the idea that factors that may contribute to the practice (such as, patterns of systemic discrimination which dis-empower women, together with advertising images which stereotype women's roles and bodies) should be radically revised or curtailed.

Clearly, a particular social practice might not be accorded the same priority when viewed from different cultural standpoints. It is possible that many women within practicing cultures see genital operations as part of a continuum of issues affecting women (including restricted access to land ownership, restricted travel, domestic violence, child marriages and short birth spacing) in the same way that many Western women may perceive self-starvation as part of a continuum of issues affecting women in Western cultures. This is not to say that either cultural practice is beyond scrutiny but, rather, to suggest that recognizing local contexts may deepen understanding about the way in which culture can influence our respective perceptions and priorities.

B. Hierarchical Relationships and Dialogue

As already suggested, it is probable that the contours of the debate about female genital operations have been influenced by power relations among and between a numbers of groups. Accordingly, any comprehensive analysis of the issues must identify and assess the impact of the relevant power imbalances on the nature of claims being made (or silenced) by these groups. Although the following list of relationships that may influence dialogue is not intended to be exhaustive.

1. Men and Women within Practicing Cultures

The relationship between men and women within practicing cultures requires careful consideration. The particular patterns of social and economic dependence which characterize the lives of many women in practicing cultures may undermine their ability to challenge cultural assumptions. This may be particularly evident where the price attached to power and status within the community is participating in the practice, a price which may, in these circumstances, be paid gladly. This, however, may be complicated by more subtle and complex factors. The symbolic meanings attached to the practice-in particular its connection to personal and communal identity-may also animate women's willingness to participate. In an attempt to incorporate this idea into a broader gender-based analysis, Cerny Smith suggests that "the ritual may actually prevent the tribal group from addressing the fact that in reality its members are not actually achieving the ritual norms; instead, one group is being oppressed by another."

2. Women from Outside and Women from within Practicing Communities

It has also been suggested that the relationship between Western and non- Western women has been influential in determining the parameters of the discussion. Harries suggests that "when Third World and Western women meet in all but the most informal of contexts, power differentials implicitly affect that relationship and shape their interaction." Outside commentators have been criticized for assuming, constructing and interpreting the experiences of women within practicing communities. Accordingly, outsiders have, in large measure, failed to fully comprehend both the complexity of meanings associated with the practices and the reactions of African women to Western criticisms of them.

3. Relationships between Cultural Groupings

Finally, any analysis should also consider the relationship between imperial powers and practicing communities and, in particular, the way this historical context influences the internal dynamics of practicing cultures.

The difficulty here lies in determining the precise role that each of these hierarchies plays in influencing the dialogue and obfuscating the reasons for the continuation of the practice. It is suggested that these contradictory claims, and the distortions engendered by these power imbalances, may be clarified by creating a space for women within practicing cultures to articulate their own experiences.

C. Struggling with Contradictions-Engaging Women from Practicing Cultures

The paradox faced by outsiders essentially amounts to this: Why do women continue to participate in a practice that threatens their health and sometimes their lives? If the practice is so horrible, why do older women who have experienced its ill-effects often insist that their daughters and granddaughters follow the tradition? By listening to the experiences and voices of women living in practicing communities, we may enrich our understanding of the multiple and overlapping ways in which different aspects of women's identities intersect. This richer understanding may, in turn, illuminate these important questions.

1. Experiencing Female Genital Operations as Empowering

Walker and Parmar document the following responses from recently circumcised women:

"It's a very happy day for us... It has been done to our mothers, and our mothers did it to us, and we will do it to our children... I don't know anything about those children and those women who haven't been circumcised. It's our tradition; maybe it's not their tradition-that's why they're not practicing it. But our tradition we will practice and we will see that it continues."

Accordingly, the practice may be experienced by women within practicing cultures as a source of empowerment, in an individual as well as a communal sense: "It can serve as a power that helps to bind the community together and provide a source of cultural identity that is often crucial in small rural communities." This attachment to the custom is consistent with Van der Kwaak's conclusion that through infibulations, Somali women acquire dignity and power "by becoming a virgin, by becoming an 'object' for which bride wealth should be paid, by being a wife, by being opened by her husband and bearing his children". Dorkenoo explains that " in many communities women's access to land and to economic resources is through the male members of the family and husbands, which implies that they cannot directly inherit land or be in control of major resources."

Even internal activists seeking to eliminate the custom are quick to point out the positive aspects of female genital operations:

"We have to learn to understand that women in a male-dominated society still come together. Through rituals, they build sisterhood-sisterhood which lasts for a long time. And these rituals are mixed with the magical, so it could be said that they are part of the control of women, that the women can be seen as custodians of male power because they prepare young women to fit into particular roles in society which are acceptable to men. But the involvement of women in organizing these magical rituals is very complex. Instead of just teaching how to be a good wife, they could be teaching women about their whole being. There is great potential in the powerful networks of women which exist in Africa. Because when girls are initiated together, they are sisters for life. Wherever you are in the world and you are in trouble, one of those sisters will come to your aid."

In some practicing communities, it is believed that "an uncircumcised woman's thoughts would constantly turn to sex and that she would do anything necessary to satisfy her lust, a behaviour completely unacceptable for a woman..." Accordingly, this might explain why some women may feel empowered by the attenuation of their sexual desire: "'This demonstrates the function of excision: it permits a woman to be mistress of her body. This is why I don't see it as a mutilation at all."'

2. Experiencing Female Genital Operations as Disempowering

Voices of dissent and despair also exist. Some women are acutely aware of the difficulties in putting an end to the custom: "'I don't know exactly how, but it does not seem to me to be impossible. At what price, I don't know. But nothing can be done towards abolition of these customs if the women concerned do not get together."' Others express uncertainty about how this might be achieved: "'I can't imagine that we would have the power to stop it. I don't have the power to stop it, but if I did, I would make it stop. because of the pain."' Still others cannot conceive of change, but explicitly articulate their experiences in terms of the disastrous consequences that could befall them or their children should they break with tradition:

"We can't afford being different. We found our mothers circumcised; we learned that our grandmothers and great-grandfathers were circumcised, and we have to carry the tradition to our children and grandchildren. We can't think of anyone who is not circumcised. Once a man divorced his wife as soon as he discovered that, out of negligence, one of her two leaves was not cut off. This man told his wife: 'What have I married? A man or a woman?' News of this incident spread and the woman did not know where to hide because of the scandal."

This sentiment is echoed in the words of Mary, a Gambian woman interviewed by Walker. When asked how she felt about the recent circumcision of her daughter she replied: "'I felt sorry for her, but I couldn't keep her, because it's the tradition and the child had to go... Here there are many events and places where a child can't go if she isn't circumcised."'

Awa Thiam sees the practice as irrefutably harmful, notwithstanding community acceptance:

"The little girl who is excised, even if she wants it because all the little girls of her age are done and because she has been persuaded, doesn't feel any less the terrifying pain. Moreover, she feels deeply the hurt done to her body. She is conscious of being wounded, diminished specifically. Whatever else may be suggested, she experiences a mutilation."

3. Situating Women's Experiences of Female Genital Operations

It is imperative to recognize that women in many practicing cultures are situated in a post-colonial context within which nationalist struggles persist. This has two important consequences. First, the impact of colonialism, particularly efforts directed at eradicating the practice, may have intensified the desire to preserve traditional rituals in order to maintain tribal identities in the face of the emergence of nation-states created by colonial powers. The desire to assert a distinct "cultural identity" in the face of undesired external intrusions may also be a factor that has contributed to a spread of the practice. In an interview with a member of the Commission for the Abolition of Sexual Mutilation in Senegal, the following observation was made:

"In Senegal in 1993, sexual mutilations are still being performed, even in circles which traditionally did not practice them previously. I have also been told that in the town of Nbour... young girls were freely offering themselves to be circumcised-even without asking their parents. Before, this mutilation was imposed on children. Now young girls offer themselves for mutilation-that is frightening."

Secondly, contemporary nationalist struggles may influence African women's perceptions of the importance and timeliness of their concerns in relation to other issues facing their communities. In the words of Dorkenoo:

" Women are often confused, because we are told that the most important issue to focus on is the nationalist struggle and that once we free ourselves from colonial domination, everything will be OK, and then we can address the women's question. When you delve into the subject, it's not just the cutting of a woman's genitals; it's also the symbolic power of it: it has implications for her psychology and character development. And therefore male-dominated society sees any attempt to change it as a threat."

The galvanizing of communities around the struggle to end imperialism is extremely important in circumstances where women who take up what is perceived to be the feminist struggle may "qualify for three 'betrayals"'-betrayal of man, woman and community. In contexts where women are economically and socially dependent on their community, the difficulties involved in "breaking ranks" is obvious. Thus, "whilst a woman may tell an interviewer that she believes a practice is wrong or ought to be different, nonetheless, she may feel her participation in the practice is necessary at least for the moment." For these reasons, Dorkenoo insists that "to be successful, campaigns on female genital mutilation should consider carefully not only eliminating but replacing the custom."

The purpose of this section has been to demonstrate two points. First, we need to acknowledge that external sources-such as colonialism-may have contributed to the practice in its current dimensions. This might be critical to furthering our understanding of the social meanings currently assigned to female genital operations by practicing communities, as well as the likely success of prevention strategies perceived as Western in origin or orientation. The second point is that women in practicing cultures may experience their culture and gender intersecting in multifarious ways, so that female genital operations can be experienced as being simultaneously empowering and oppressive. Framing appropriate solutions, therefore, "requires an acknowledgement of, and co-operation with, the different sources of power which affect women in different ways".

INTERNAL DEBATE AND EXTERNAL CRITIQUE-APPLYING INTERNATIONAL HUMAN-RIGHTS STANDARDS

Developing a deeper understanding of the significance and complexities of female genital operations is critical to the process of uncovering shared values and norms turn now to the role of international human-rights norms and procedures in this process.

A. Internal Debate-The Transformative Potential of Human-Rights Norms

Despite the limitations of human-rights norms as embodiments of universal morality, many states have expressed their commitment to the standards of conduct outlined by them. International human-rights norms also provide the advantage of a common language through which minority voices can articulate their concerns to their local communities and to the international community. Accordingly, the inter-penetration of ideas between cultures may be facilitated by international instruments that have the potential to spark or animate internal debates. Harries suggests: "Through this process, internationally defined rights are given a certain localized, ideological context."

While female genital operations have been variously analyzed by outsider scholars as a violation of the right to be free from discriminatory practices, the right to be free from torture or cruel, inhuman or degrading treatment, the right to sexual and corporeal integrity and the right to health, vigorous internal debates surrounding the practices have also adopted the language of rights. The next section deals with the use of international human-rights standards in internal discussions about female genital operations.

1. Discrimination Against Women and Children

C.E.D.A.W. obliges state parties to take all appropriate measures to modify the social and cultural patterns of conduct of men and women, with a view to achieving the elimination of prejudices and customary and all other practices which are based on the idea of the inferiority or superiority of either of the sexes or on stereotyped roles for men and women.

Burkina Faso, Egypt, Ethiopia, Gambia, Guinea, Senegal, Nigeria, Mali and Kenya have ratified the C.E.D.A.W., whilst Djibouti, Somalia and Sudan (where some of the highest rates of female genital operations are recorded) have not. All of the above-mentioned states, however, have ratified the African Charter of Human and Peoples' Rights, which specifies that, "the State shall ensure the elimination of every discrimination against women and also censure the protection of the rights of the woman and the child as stipulated in international declarations and conventions."

The applicability of the C.E.D.A.W. to female genital operations depends on the extent to which these practices are seen to be based on the belief that women are inferior or on stereotyped roles for women. Thomas Sunkara, the former President of Burkina Faso, has made this connection quite explicitly:

When a man takes his daughter or his daughters for excision, independently of any cultural and mystical values he wishes and tries to impart to his act, there is a clear difference in the care he shows for his small sons who go to be circumcised and the care, or rather the contempt, disdain and disregard he shows for his daughters in handing them over to undergo a form of butchery.

It also shows an attempt to confer an inferior status on women by branding them with this mark which diminishes them and is a constant reminder to them that they are only women, inferior to men, that they do not even have any rights over their own bodies or to fulfilment either bodily or personal. They have limits imposed on them by men.

As we can view circumcision as being a measure of hygiene, in the same way we can only see excision as a measure of inferiorization.

As I will explain in the following section, however, the framing of the issues by outsider critics in these terms (particularly regarding women's rights over their own bodies) has been controversial. At this stage, it is also important to note that the practices have been challenged by internal critics in these terms.

2. Right to Health

The United Nations Convention on the Rights of the Child states: "States Parties shall take all effective and appropriate measures with a view to abolishing traditional practices prejudicial to the health of children." Burkina Faso, Egypt, Ethiopia, Gambia, Guinea, Senegal, Nigeria, Mali and Kenya have ratified the Children's Convention, although Somalia has not. Again, all the above-mentioned states have ratified the African Charter, which specifies:

i. Every individual shall have the right to enjoy the best attainable state of physical and mental health.
ii. States parties to the present Charter shall take the necessary measures to protect the health of their people and to ensure that they receive medical attention when they are sick.

In terms of the health consequences of female genital operations, the immediate physical effects of infibulation include "damage to the urethral meatus, Bartholin's glands, the perineum and possibly the rectum," depending on the level of resistance of the child. Additional complications include: haemorrhage (the clitoris has a rich arterial blood supply), shock from pain and blood loss, septicaemia, infection of the wound and internal reproductive organs (tetanus is a real threat due to unsterile instruments), urine retention due to occlusion, damage to and bleeding from adjacent tissues and organs and death. H.I.V. transmission is also a possibility.

The long-term physical effects of infibulation have also been documented. These include:

Urinary tract infections, menstruation difficulty, sterility, extensive malformation and scarring (including vulvar abscesses, epidermoid inclusion cysts, and keloids), pain from reopening the infibulation with a knife on the wedding night, and difficult penetration by the sexual partner. The circumcised female may also experience difficulties giving birth, [including] prolonged labor, perinea and deep trauma, and rupture of the uterus which may also result in fetal death or brain damage.

Dr. Kouyate describes the long-term complications based on her experience:

"The woman has been cut and traumatized, so intercourse is very painful and there are a lot of problems giving birth. An area which is normally elastic has become a cicatrix area. As a result, many women tear, at the top and at the bottom. If they are in hospital, you can perform an episiotomy, you can enlarge the opening. But just imagine these women who have to give birth at home... They are just left with a tear at the top and bottom, at the top causing massive hemorrhaging, at the bottom even worse-the tear can enlarge to the anus, so that women can no longer contain their feces.... Not only are women affected, but babies are affected, too."

Dorkenoo and Elworthy report that members of the medical profession in Egypt, Somalia, Sudan, Kenya, Djibouti, Mali, Nigeria, Burkina Faso, Ghana and the Ivory Coast have spoken out about the harmful consequences of female genital operations. In reference to the results of a survey of forty-three Sudanese gynecologists, they state:

All agreed that any form of mutilation was bound to create medical complications. Every respondent believed that it was a harmful and unnecessary practice and that an effort should be put to end it. They were unanimous that a wide campaign of publicity was needed, showing not only the dangers of mutilations but also the erroneous belief that it was required by religion.

The Inter-African Committee on Traditional Practices Affecting the Health of Women and Children was established in 1984 and has focused on the issue of female genital operations. Twenty-four affiliated African committees have since been established to develop and co-ordinate strategies and plans to eradicate female genital operations. The Sudan National Committee on Harmful Traditional Practices, for example, has been involved in activities ranging from the education and training of health workers and traditional birth attendants (who commonly perform the practice), establishing alternative employment programmes for traditional practitioners and initiating consulting workshops with a broad range of community group leaders.

B. Translating Principle into Action-Internal Initiatives and Strategies

One example of how international human-rights norms might be incorporated into strategies for change at the local level is illustrated in the following extract from a lecture given by Zainaba (a local nurse) to the midwives of Touil, Mauritania:

"The Way of the Prophet... tells us that women should be circumcised. It is not a sin if it is not done, but it is better if it is. In any case it is said that the matter in which it should be performed is that one third of the clitoris should be cut off and two thirds should be left intact. Someone who practically attacks a girl with a knife, cutting off everything... is, in any case, going directly against the words of the Prophet... (Disturbed chatter, 'I didn't know...') God created woman to be with man. He created her to be his wife so that they could help each other. It is not right if only the man has feeling and the women feel nothing. That is a great sin. After all, a man and a wife are from the same tribes aren't they, and people from the same tribe should always work together and help each other, shouldn't they?... If a woman's entire clitoris is cut off, it leaves her cold, lazy, without interest, humourless. Doing that is like killing her, it is a sin....

"You all must not, as is your custom, rush into a family's tent when they call you to circumcise their daughter saying, 'Give me the child, give me the razor blade and get my payment ready!' First you must clean everything. Today we are teaching you to be nurses-we will give each of you medication and explain how to use it all... When you go back to your villages, you have a duty. You must be an example of cleanliness and health to everyone..."

Significantly, Zainaba did not attempt to invalidate the practice, for to do so may have been completely unacceptable to her and her audience. She does, however, challenge the midwives to use their power responsibly in the interests of women. Oram observes that:

> In light of the fact that Maures believe so strongly in female circumcision, Zainaba's lecture presented the traditional midwives with a challenge. This challenge was made even more poignant because Zainaba is both a Maure and a woman... As a Maure, Zainaba is part of the culture that she is trying to change. She is a Muslim, herself circumcised. She is subject to the beliefs and pressures of Maure society just as the midwives are.

Instead, Zainaba concentrated her efforts on ensuring that the physical intervention was minimized, by invoking well-recognized and respected norms and authority such as the word of the Prophet, community cooperation and duties to the community. By emphasizing critical connections between the ways in which the operation is performed, the overall physical and mental health of women and children and God's will, she was able to persuade the midwives of the seriousness and importance of taking care in performing their operations. Her presentation not only underscores the importance of women's health, but also the "sinfulness" of discriminatory treatment: "It is not right if only the man has feeling and the women feel nothing." She is engaging in what An-Na'im calls an "internal struggle for control over the cultural sources and symbols of power within that society." It may be that the traditional practitioners could accept her directions because she is able to legitimize them by using powerful cultural symbols. By analyzing Zainaba's approach, outsiders may develop a sharper insight into the cross- cultural content of human-rights standards relating to health and discrimination.

However, tension persists. For those internal critics who wish to see the practices completely eradicated, the strong focus on the health aspects insidiously obscures the systemic factors that underlie the practices and prevents these from being adequately addressed. Dorkenoo has observed:

"Genital mutilation is basically a social practice, with a health consequence. Generally, people have been dealing with it on the health side, and my impression is that if you don't get to the roots, which are the social meaning of it, we will never be able to deal with it."

This dilemma is evident in the recent controversy over female genital operations in Egypt. In 1994, the Egyptian Health Minister pledged the government's commitment to eradicating female genital operations at the International Conference on Population and Development. This provoked a strong reaction from leaders in the Muslim community, culminating in the promulgation of an edict by the Grand Sheikh of Cairo's Al-Azhar University which stipulated that female genital operations were a duty for all Muslim women. In response, the Egyptian government significantly relaxed its position on female genital operations by permitting the practice in public hospitals. This course was justified on the grounds that performing the practice under medically controlled conditions would minimize the health risk involved.

On the question of medicalizing the practice, Dorkenoo and Elworthy state:

The tendency to "clean up" the gory aspects of the operations by either offering to perform them in hospitals, or by providing midwives and other operators with anaesthetics and penicillin... [for the purpose of]... sanitizing the custom, and thus effectively removing the health based objections, must be refused.

This is consistent with the approach adopted by the Inter-African Committee on Traditional Practices Affecting the Health of Women and Children ("I.A.C.T.P."). The I.A.C.T.P. has established a task force for the purpose of developing strategies for combating the practice in Egypt, which do not involve medicalization as an intermediate measure. The main question, in the face of these internal tensions, is how to determine the appropriate role and form of external criticism.

C. The Role of External Criticism

As indicated in Part I, above, An-Na'im theorizes that external criticism of a cultural practice or belief is most likely to be effective when made in support of the "proponents of enlightened perceptions" within a culture and framed in a manner consistent with internal values. Statements made by a range of African spokes-people support this view.

Like all other practices that oppress African women, genital mutilation must be fought against. But the priorities and the weapons used in the battle must be chosen by Africans themselves, and more especially by women. For these practices will not disappear of their own accord for a very long time... Outside support can only be effective and perceived as non-imperialist if it takes as its starting point informational and educational activities necessarily carried out in each country.

Similarly, Abdoul Diouf, in his capacity as President of Senegal, stated: "The main part of this struggle will be waged by education rather than by anathema and from the inside rather than from the outside."

This point has also been made in international fora. For example, paragraph 45 of the "Review and Evaluation of Progress Achieved in the Implementation of the (1975) World Plan of Action: Health", considered at the 1980 United Nations Women's Conference in Copenhagen, states:

Female circumcision and infibulation can lead to complications during pregnancy. The Second Regional Conference on the Integration of Women in Development... condemned sexual mutilation practices, but was also critical of uninformed international campaigns against these practices, and called upon Governments and women's organizations to seek solutions to the problem.

These criticisms have focused, in particular, on Western characterizations of the practice as a violation of the "right" of women to control their bodies and sexuality. Some Western critics have contended that the practice violates the right to sexual and corporeal integrity on the grounds that it is performed for the purpose of suppressing sexual drive and has the effect of degrading and impairing women's sexual organs and of subjugating women generally. These approaches have, in some circumstances, been met with antipathy and rejection by African women. Boulware-Miller points out:

> The response to the sexual and corporal integrity argument is that the term "mutilation" is disrespectful of African women who have been circumcised. While advocates... use the word "mutilation" to express their outrage at the practice, in so describing an important part of African women's cultural identity, they offend all Africans.

Allegations of Western insensitivity and imperialism inevitably arise in this context:

> The aggressive nature of the campaign, the insensitive attitude towards a different culture, the paternalism and activism displayed have left us shocked and enraged. The campaign has been undertaken on the basis of Western prejudices-the mentality of the "centre"-themselves founded uniquely on the morals and culture of the Christian West. In their desire to stir the passions of the general public in the West, the men and women responsible have forgotten that they might be damaging the self- respect of every woman they are setting out to "save", by destroying the foundations of their beliefs.

The force of these criticisms, together with the pragmatic belief that health-based strategies are likely to be the most successful, has led some commentators to conclude that health-based approaches are the most appropriate. By confining criticism to principles, such as the right to health, and strategies, such as education, the backlash against Western interference may be minimized. External agents are not then seen to be imposing their will on unique cultural contexts. Moreover, this approach can be more easily integrated into existing values and social and economic priorities. Harries, for example, reports that local legislation mandating female excision in the Kapchworo district of Uganda remained in effect, notwithstanding condemnation by government officials. Yet, subsequent educational campaigns informing men about the dangers of the practice have reversed attitudes in some cases, leading an increasing number of men to prevent their daughters from being circumcised. Most importantly, focusing on health and education approaches does not tend to place women in the position of having to "choose" between enforcing "substantively hollow rights" and remaining part of an extant social structure that rejects those rights.

However, as recent proposals to medicalize the practice indicate, the health-based objections may not adequately cover the field. Ironically, Egypt's proposal might be viewed as being consistent with health-based objectives. In this case, the appropriate form of external criticism must not only draw attention to Egypt's international obligations under C.E.D.A.W., but must underscore the right of all women to be free from discriminatory practices, in addition to their right to health. This approach would lend support to the dissenting Egyptian groups that initiated efforts to challenge the Egyptian government's proposal to allow the practice to be performed in public hospitals. The recent reversal in Egypt's position implies that this form of protest can be effective.

It is suggested that the health-based objections to the practices have had, and continue to have, the effect of raising consciousness within practicing communities about the health dangers associated with the practice. Ongoing discussion holds the potential to further inform the processes of changing local conditions and perceptions, so that the practices may be effectively challenged on a variety of grounds. It may be, for instance, that the impetus for challenging the practices as violent and discriminatory may gain greater prominence after the health concerns have been widely discussed and largely confirmed. The internal debate surrounding Egypt's proposals may be a case in point. This demonstrates that cross-cultural dialogue is a process in constant flux and, accordingly, should be subject to constant revision as cross-cultural understandings expand and internal re- interpretations of cultural norms change local conditions.

D. An Assessment of the Participatory Role of International Bodies

An examination of the work of United Nations bodies and conferences evidences the tensions discussed above. It also illustrates the way in which cross-cultural dialogue on this issue has evolved in response to those tensions. For a long time, United Nations agencies declined to examine the practice. In 1984, however, amid growing international concern and pressure from women's groups, the United Nations Sub-Commission on the Prevention of Discrimination and the Protection of Minorities established a working group to investigate and report on traditional practices affecting the health of women and children.

Significantly, the Working Group on Traditional Practices Affecting the Health of Women and Children analyzed female genital operations "from a cultural and historical perspective as well as from a human rights perspective".

In particular, the working group focused on how female genital operations, as a rite of passage and as a test for women's capacity to endure acute suffering, operate as cultural justifications for the practice. This has led one commentator to conclude that the working group perceived its task as a balancing act between the harmful health consequences of female genital operations and the cultural significance of the practice.

This may explain the Working Group's reticence on the question of whether the practice constitutes a violation of human-rights. The Working Group concluded that the custom had serious physical and psychological health consequences and was "at variance" with human-rights standards. It did not, however, specifically enumerate which human-rights standards the practice contravenes. According to Brennan, the Working Group's conclusion was influenced by opposition to the practice within practicing communities, evidence that the initiatory aspects of the practice were diminishing in significance and the ratification of international human-rights instruments.

Although the Report of the Working Group failed to state which human-rights standards prohibited the practice, the Sub-Commission subsequently adopted a resolution that the practice was a violation of the "rights of women and children". According to Brennan, the Sub-Commission preferred to support internal efforts to eradicate the practice-based on education and persuasion-rather than coercing governments into taking active steps to prohibit female genital operations.

On the one hand, the Report of the Working Group, the processes leading to its creation and the Sub-Commission's response, constitute a good example of how cultural sensitivities can be incorporated into international discussions. The approach adopted emphasized the importance of consultation with members from practicing countries in an effort to understand the cultural significance of the practices. It also recognized the importance of recommending action that underscores the internal struggles surrounding the practice rather than concentrating on external pressure. This preference for broad education efforts has the added advantage of placing female genital operations in an organic context, as one issue in a continuum of health concerns for African women.

On the other hand, the Report of the Working Group has been criticized for not adequately addressing the gender dimension of female genital operations. The focus on cultural significance, at the expense of gender inequities, oversimplified the analysis and prevented the working group from addressing concerns about discrimination and the control of women's sexuality. It also circumvented the obvious need to examine other factors that may contribute to the continuation of the practice such as the economic dependence of women, nor did it address questions about empowering women in practicing communities so that their voices and priorities may be heard.

The international discussion, however, has continued to evolve in light of greater participation from men and women from practicing cultures, changing the perceptions and the re-interpretation of internal norms. More recent international efforts to address female genital operations are incorporated in the "Programme of Action" adopted by the International Conference on Population and Development, and the "Platform for Action" adopted by the Fourth World Conference on Women. Although neither document is legally binding, each, nonetheless, evidences a commitment by participating governments to the principles and recommendations enumerated therein.

The Cairo Programme of Action, focusing on the health and educational aspects of the practices, states:

Governments and communities should urgently take steps to stop the practice of female genital mutilation and protect women and girls from all such similar unnecessary and dangerous practices. Steps to eliminate the practice should include strong community outreach programs involving village and religious leaders, education and counselling about its impact on girls' and women's health, and appropriate treatment and rehabilitation for girls and women who have suffered mutilation. Services should include counseling for women and men to discourage the practice.

Elsewhere in the Programme, however, the violent and discriminatory nature of the practice is addressed, and the following recommendation is made: "Governments should take effective action to eliminate all forms of coercion and discrimination in policies and practices. Measures should be adopted and enforced to eliminate female genital mutilation."

The Beijing Platform for Action addresses female genital operations under the categories of "Women and Health" and "Violence Against Women." While health concerns and educational strategies remain important priorities, the document also regards the practice as a form of discrimination against women and specifically characterizes it as a form of violence against women:

The term "violence against women" means any act of gender-based violence that results in, or is likely to result in, physical, sexual or psychological harm or suffering to women, including threats of such acts, coercion or arbitrary deprivation of liberty, whether occurring in public or private life.

Accordingly, violence against women encompasses but is not limited to the following:... female genital mutilation and other traditional practices harmful to women...

The Platform also includes substantive recommendations that aim to translate these principles into action. In relation to health and education, the Platform recommends that governments Live priority to formal and informal educational programmes that support and enable women to develop self-esteem, acquire knowledge, make decisions on and take responsibility for their own health, achieve mutual respect in matters concerning sexuality and fertility and educate men regarding the importance of women's health and well-being, placing special focus on programmes for both men and women that emphasise the elimination of harmful attitudes and practices, including female genital mutilation...

Governments enact and enforce legislation against the perpetrators of practices and acts of violence against women, such as female genital mutilation... and give vigorous support to the efforts of non-governmental and community organizations to eliminate such practices.

On the one hand, these recommendations appropriately demonstrate an appreciation of existing tensions between cultural sensitivity and international human-rights standards. They support the efforts of some internal critics and activists who are challenging the practice in their communities, by using strong language to criticize the practices as a manifestation of violence and discrimination. At the same time, the reaffirmation of the importance of health- and education-based strategies, together with the focus on encouraging the efforts of grass-roots organizations, ensures that those who are best placed to incorporate the experiences of women from practicing cultures will be significant participants in program planning. This is fundamental to ensuring that the women most affected by the practices are not alienated from the constantly evolving cross-cultural dialogue.

CONCLUSION

What have been attempted to demonstrate is that by taking a dynamic view of culture as a series of ongoing internal and external debates, the role of cross-cultural dialogue in expanding cross-cultural understandings of human rights looks promising. I have argued that this approach opens up opportunities for discourse by orienting us to the cultural and historical assumptions that inform human-rights debate. The methodology proposed encourages us to re-evaluate theoretical positions and strategies in light of the actual (rather than imagined or imposed) experiences and priorities of those with the cultural tools to devise the best strategies for dealing with human-rights concerns.

The customary practice of female genital operations has attracted considerable attention and criticism from commentators outside practicing cultures. For a longer time, internal commentators have been addressing the issues arising from these practices within their communities. In response to these internal and external processes (sometimes reflective, sometimes ill- informed) a cross-cultural dialogue has emerged. The centering of women's experiences is a necessary part of this dialogue for the following reasons. First, with this perspective, outsider assertions about the nature and reasons for continuation of the practice can be tested and, perhaps, challenged. Secondly, we can appreciate the form and content of the internal struggles and debates surrounding the issue. Finally, we might subsequently engage in a form of criticism that supports those internal agitators in culturally appropriate ways.

International human rights norms can play a critical role in facilitating and animating both internal and external criticism of cultural practices. Both outsider and insider commentators have adopted the language of rights to articulate their criticisms of the practice. However, the particular "rights" relied upon and the reactions to these claims have varied among and between outsiders and insiders. In recent times, the health-based objections to the practice have been preferred because the discrimination-based objections have been criticized for failing to appreciate local norms and perceptions.

Outsider criticism that is insensitive to local contexts may indeed be ultimately counter-productive by undermining the efforts of internal critics seeking to gain cultural legitimacy for their position; but this does not mean that outsiders have no valuable contribution. From the perspective of an outsider, argued that focusing exclusively on the health-based aspects of the practices is undesirable. While health-based analyses of female genital operations are less challenging to cultural (and patriarchal) sensitivities, they may also be less likely in the long term to effectively integrate women's experiences of injustice into human-rights law.

This focus may also have the undesired effect of displacing critical questions about the social meaning of female genital operations and their role in controlling female sexuality. These concerns have been raised by women within practicing cultures and require closer examination. I have suggested that the terms of cross-cultural dialogue should be subject to constant revision as cross- cultural understandings expand and internal re-interpretations of cultural norms change local conditions. This means that criticism, comment and strategies that are inappropriate at one stage in the process of dialogue will not necessarily always be so.

4

Maternal Mortality, Population Control, and the War in Women's Wombs

Quinacrine hydrochloride is a drug that was developed in the late 1920's to prevent and treat malaria. It is also used to treat several other diseases including giardiasis, lupus, and rheumatoid arthritis. Given its history, it is hard to imagine how this drug became notoriously known as a female sterilization agent. In the past three decades, two American doctors, Elton Kessel and Stephen Mumford, have been the main proponents of a worldwide quinacrine sterilization crusade. As a result of their crusade, approximately 104,410 women in nineteen developing countries have already been subjected to quinacrine sterilizations. This Chapter raises questions regarding the ethics of promoting quinacrine sterilizations even though quinacrine has not been approved for sterilization purposes by any government agency in the world.

BACKGROUND AND HISTORICAL INFORMATION ABOUT QUINACRINE STERILIZATIONS

Quinacrine was first used for sterilization in the early 1970s by Dr. Jaime Zipper, a Chilean researcher. Dr. Zipper performed approximately four thousand sterilizations of Chilean women until the Chilean government banned the procedure in 1998, after reports of its cancer causing potential and alleged misuse.

In his earliest phase of experimentation, Dr. Zipper injected quinacrine into women's uteruses in liquid form. This quinacrine concoction was referred to as the quinacrine slurry. Due to its high failure rate (approximately 35%) and because three women died as a result of exposure to quinacrine slurries, Dr. Zipper developed the quinacrine pellet. In pellet form, quinacrine is inserted through the vagina into the uterus with a tool similar to that used to insert intra-uterine devices (IUDs). Within thirty minutes, the quinacrine pellets dissolve and liquid quinacrine then travels through the fallopian tubes, causing an injury similar to a chemical burn. Over the next six to twelve weeks, the burn-like injury in the fallopian tubes turns into scar tissue, which in turn blocks anything from getting in and out of the uterus, thereby causing permanent sterilization. Although the procedure is often painful and uncomfortable, quinacrine sterilizations are performed without anesthesia. Many women faint as a result of the pain.

Although the long-term side effects of quinacrine sterilizations are not yet known, what has been reported is that this non surgical form of sterilization has caused burning and irritation of the vaginal walls, cervical stenosis (a narrowing of the cervical opening), uterine adhesions, excitation of the central nervous system, toxic psychosis, and perforation of the uterus. Abnormal menstrual bleeding, backaches, fever, lower abdominal pain and headaches have also been reported. In addition, if the quinacrine sterilization is not properly performed, incomplete blockage of the fallopian tubes could occur, thereby causing an ectopic pregnancy - a life-threatening emergency, particularly in areas with no emergency medical facilities for surgery.

The risks associated with fetal exposure to quinacrine are also unknown. There is, however, one reported case of an anencephalic infant conceived two and a half months following intrauterine insertion of quinacrine in a Vietnamese woman, and one reported case of a hydrocephalic infant being born to a woman who had previously undergone quinacrine sterilization. In addition to birth defects, there is concern regarding the excretion of quinacrine hydrocholoride into breast milk because the effects of quinacrine on breastfed infants are also unknown.

Studies show that between two and five of every one hundred chemically sterilized women become pregnant after one year. Consequently, there is a need for follow-up studies to be done in order to track the effects of quinacrine on infants and developing fetuses.

Quinacrine pellets have not been adequately tested or approved for use as a sterilization agent anywhere in the world. Many major family planning organizations and foreign governments, as well as the World Health Organization, oppose its use for sterilization. Despite this fact, quinacrine is being distributed worldwide by two U.S. organizations - a North Carolina organization called the Center for Research on Population and Security and the International Federation for Family Health, run by Stephen Mumford and Elton Kessel respectively. These organizations are the only distributors of quinacrine in the world.

THE KESSEL AND MUMFORD QUINACRINE CRUSADE

Dr. Elton Kessel is a Harvard and University of Chicago trained medical doctor and public health consultant from Carlton, Oregon and is eighty years old. He is the former director of Family Health International (FHI), a non-profit agency that funded Dr. Zipper's quinacrine research in Chile during the 1970's. News reports indicate that he left FHI over differences about both the reporting and the conduct of quinacrine sterilization clinical trials. His partner, Stephen Mumford, was also an employee of FHI at one point. Three years after Kessel was fired, Mumford was dismissed for writing a string of chapters blaming the Vatican for the United States' failure to adopt a policy classifying population growth in the Third World as a threat to the national security of the United States.

Mumford is not a medical doctor. He is fifty seven years old and holds a doctorate in Health Sciences Administration and Population Studies. He began his career promoting contraception and population control. For the past two decades, Mumford's fervor has focused on female sterilization through the use of quinacrine. Mumford and Kessel joined forces in 1984 after Mumford incorporated the Center for Research on Population and Security. Together, Mumford and Kessel have distributed quinacrine in nineteen countries including Bangladesh, Chile, China, Colombia, Costa Rica, Croatia, Egypt, India, Indonesia, Iran, Morocco, Pakistan, the Philippines, Venezuela, Vietnam, the United States, Malaysia and Romania.

In a remarkably quiet crusade, Mumford and Kessel have paid for the manufacture of quinacrine in Switzerland, arranged for its distribution in about twenty countries and mobilized a network of doctors, nurses and midwives to administer it. Most of the sterilizations are a result of free donations or gifts of quinacrine given by Mumford and Kessel to doctors and health practitioners all over the world. In 1997, the worldwide efforts of Mumford's center cost only $156,000. Apparently, neither Mumford nor Kessel seek financial gain from this endeavor. In fact, Mumford draws a salary of only $37,500 a year from his research center, and Kessel reportedly lives off less than $30,000 from Social Security and income from small investments. As Morley Safer, co-host of 60 Minutes pointed out: "Or them, quinacrine is not a job, it's a crusade."

FUNDING OF THE QUINACRINE CAMPAIGN

Private funding from the Leland Fikes Foundation and the Scaife Family Foundation, have made it possible for Mumford and Kessel to provide quinacrine free of charge to researchers, clinicians, and government health agencies worldwide. Mumford and Kessel's gifts of quinacrine are made possible not only through the right-wing Leland Fikes and Scaife Family Foundations but also through the financial support of individuals such as Sarah G. Epstein and Donald Collins, both board members of the Federation for American

Immigration Reform (FAIR), a conservative, anti-immigrant organization.

Like his financial supporters, Mumford also embraces an anti-immigration agenda. He is quoted as stating: "This explosion in human numbers, which after 2050 will come entirely from immigrants and the offspring of immigrants, will dominate our lives. There will be chaos and anarchy." He has also been quoted as saying that quinacrine is "essential to population-growth control" and that "overpopulation is a gravely serious national security issue, even more serious than the nuclear threat." Mumford's promotion of quinacrine is also steeped in the belief that quinacrine is an ideal method of population control because it is a cheap nonsurgical sterilization method that requires no operating room, no anesthesia, no expensive equipment and no lengthy training. In fact, Mumford claims that quinacrine is the best contraceptive for the world's poorest women because it costs less than one dollar and is so simple a procedure that it can be performed in very modest settings by trained "nonphysicians." He claims that quinacrine is safer than surgical sterilization in countries where hospitals and clinics are poorly equipped. For this reason, quinacrine supporters often refer to it as the most revolutionary birth control development since the pill. They say it has the potential for curbing rampant population growth in developing countries, and they claim it can save the lives of millions of women who cannot obtain contraceptives or safe surgical sterilizations and would otherwise die as a result of unwanted childbearing. According to Elton Kessel, quinacrine "will save more lives of women of reproductive age around the world than anything else we have."

QUINACRINE ABUSE AND SAFETY CONCERNS

Opponents of quinacrine, however, point out that the potential for abuse is horrifying because quinacrine is simple to administer, irreversible, and inexpensive. In an chapter in the May 29, 1989, edition of the International Journal of Gynaecology and Obstetrics, Elton Kessel acknowledged that one of the most intriguing features of quinacrine is that it can be used to accomplish sterilization on a massive scale. Kessel argued that if the method were introduced in India's national family planning program, one million additional sterilization procedures could be performed there every year. Approximately one year after the International Journal of Gynecology and Obstetrics had predicted quinacrine's potential for abuse, actual abuse of quinacrine sterilizations in India, as well as several other countries, was reported.

The Indian government eventually banned quinacrine, claiming that after six years of "illegal" clinical trials, the government was concerned about the complications caused by quinacrine sterilizations, including fetal abnormalities and cancer of the uterus. The Indian government was not alone in expressing concern regarding the side effects and toxicity of quinacrine. In fact, many doctors expressed concern that quinacrine may be a carcinogenic. The concerns regarding carcinogenicity are based on laboratory studies indicating that quinacrine causes cells to mutate. According to some scientists, mutagenicity is circumstantial evidence of cancer.

In addition, other studies indicate that quinacrine causes DNA damage to bacteria, which is a prima facie case that quinacrine may cause cancer in human beings. The FDA has indicated that because intrauterine administration of quinacrine pellets will result in significant tissue damage in the presence of a known mutagen, "serious concerns exist that such exposure could result in development of cancer of the reproductive tract." This concern appears to be valid, particularly in light of the fact that a retrospective study of 421 Chilean women who had undergone quinacrine sterilization between 1977 and 1982 revealed a cluster of nine cases of cancer. A second retrospective study of 1,492 Chilean women revealed that there were a total of seventeen cases of invasive cancer, including higher than expected numbers of breast and cervical cancer for that population. Despite the fact that questions of safety and effectiveness have not been resolved, and despite the fact that quinacrine sterilizations have not been approved by the FDA, Kessel and Mumford have solicited abortion providers in the United States to perform quinacrine sterilization. According to Kessel, official government approval through the FDA would have been "desirable but not necessary" because the FDA permits approved drugs to be used "off-label." Kessel argues that since quinacrine is an approved drug for treating malaria, doctors should be free to prescribe quinacrine for any purpose, including sterilization. Thus, Mumford concludes that it is "legal for clinicians to perform this procedure on American women as an off-label use of an approved drug."

The FDA, however, disagreed. In October 1998, it ordered Kessel and Mumford to destroy their existing supply of quinacrine tablets and to immediately stop all export and distribution of the drug. The FDA stated that quinacrine used for sterilizations was an "unapproved new drug and a misbranded drug in violation of the Federal Food, Drug, and Cosmetic Act." It also indicated that quinacrine pellets used for non-surgical female sterilizations was an "unsafe use of this drug product." Finally, the FDA stated that it was "very concerned about the safety risks associated with the use of this drug and its effects on women and the fetus if a woman is or becomes pregnant."

The FDA warned Kessel and Mumford that if they did not "immediately halt" distribution of the quinacrine pellets, they could face possible seizure of the pellets or criminal prosecution. In addition to forbidding the marketing of quinacrine in the United States for sterilization purposes, the Warning Letter forbade the import of the drug into the United States under sections 301(a) and (d) of the Food, Drug, and Cosmetic Act (FDCA). The FDA also warned Dr. Mumford that under section 801, a product may only be exported to another country if it complies with the laws of that country and has valid marketing authorization by the appropriate authority. The letter concluded that since quinacrine is not approved for use in non-surgical sterilizations in any country listed under the Act, exporting the drug would violate the Act.

On September 24, 1998, during a telephone conversation between Mumford and the FDA, a FDA agent asked Mumford to identify the location of his remaining inventory of quinacrine, consisting of approximately 290,000 quinacrine pellets and 1,536 filled inserters. Specifically, the FDA requested that Mumford "immediately halt all distribution of any and all quinacrine... identify its location, and voluntarily destroy it under FDA supervision." Mumford chose not to provide the FDA with the location of the products. He also announced that, if necessary, he would escape the jurisdiction of the FDA by finding someone outside of the United States to distribute it. From September 1998 until December 1999, little was written about Mumford and Kessel's quinacrine escapades. The future of quinacrine sterilizations laid in abeyance until Warren Buffet, the self-made billionaire investment guru, revived quinacrine research by donating two million dollars to FHI. With this two million dollar donation, FHI will resume animal testing and begin human testing of quinacrine sterilizations in preparation for FDA approval. Planned Parenthood Federation of America, the largest reproductive health-care organization in the United States, has defended quinacrine sterilizations, indicating that they are willing to test quinacrine on their patients. Commentators predict that large scale human clinical trials of quinacrine may begin as early as 2002 in the United States. In the meantime, Jack Lippes, Professor Emeritus at the University of Buffalo Medical School, has received approval from the Children's Hospital of Buffalo to conduct quinacrine sterilization on ten women.

ETHICAL STANDARDS GOVERNING HUMAN EXPERIMENTATION

Unfortunately, the quinacrine sterilization campaign is just one of several examples of human experimentation where poor women particularly women of color have been used as guinea pigs in the name of advancing reproductive technology. In the early stages of developing the oral contraceptive pill, for example, women in Puerto Rico were used as subjects to determine the pill's safety and effectiveness. Many of the 132 women in Puerto Rico who were part of the early experiment died as a direct result of using the pill. Those who did not die suffered a variety of side effects, including cancer, urinary infections, weight loss or gain, depression, irritability, nausea, vomiting, and unexplained changes in menstrual periods.

In the early clinical trials for Norplant, women of color living in Asia, the Pacific, Latin America and Africa reported that they were not adequately informed of side effects. Many of the doctors participating in the clinical trials assured women that Norplant was "totally" safe, even though the doctors did not know the long-term side effects and the effects that Norplant would have on women who were breast-feeding. In one study, where primarily poor Egyptian women were test subjects, women reported that they experienced severe depression, weight loss, headaches and heavy bleeding.

After the clinical testing was concluded and Norplant was approved by the FDA, many women requested that their doctors remove Norplant from their bodies due to various side effects. They were told, however, that removal was not an option. Due to the long list of health complications and the difficulties associated with having Norplant removed, several women filed class action lawsuits in Texas, Illinois, and Florida. Over 50,000 women eventually filed complaints.

Like the pill and Norplant, doctors first tested the Dalkon Shield (an intrauterine device designed in 1968) on poor women of color. This time, the women of choice were African-American women from Baltimore. Many of the women involved in this experiment contracted a serious life-threatening uterine infection known as pelvic inflammatory disease. By 1975, women filed several hundred lawsuits against the Dalkon Shield manufacturer claiming a long list of injuries including death related to spontaneous septic abortion, perforations of the uterus, ectopic pregnancies and pregnancies associated with birth defects. By 1984, over 7,000 Dalkon Shield lawsuits had settled at a cost of $260 million while 3,500 cases were still pending. Eventually, the manufacturer of the Dalkon Shield filed for bankruptcy in order to avoid paying the costs associated with litigation.

The history of women as human subjects in experiments involving reproductive technology indicates that the rights of women are often abused. Women are told very little about the potential side effects of the drugs or devices that are being used in their bodies. Doctors provide very little, if any, information regarding alternatives to the new drugs and devices. Often doctors approach women who "choose" to use new reproductive technologies when they are at their most vulnerable. In Namibia, for example, in the 1980s, Depo-Provera was the most accessible contraceptive. Women interviewed in the black townships of Katatura, Ovamboland, and Kavango indicated that hospital personnel gave them injections immediately after childbirth regardless of their medical history and sometimes against their will. Similarly, young black women in South Carolina and Chicago, Illinois reported that immediately after giving birth, they were pressured into "consenting" to use either Norplant or Depo-Provera.

In the case of quinacrine, women from all over the developing world have been sterilized by a drug whose long-term side effects and effects on fetuses are unknown. In many cases informed consent was not obtained or honored; and therefore, these women were subjected to quinacrine sterilizations against their will. When one looks at this issue in combination with the history of sterilization as a form of population control, it is difficult to simply discard the quinacrine campaign as an unfortunate but necessary occurrence for the advancement of gynecological science.

With such serious allegations of violations of informed consent, as well as other ethical breaches, it seems as if something should be done to ensure that further abuse in quinacrine research does not occur. Although international codes of ethics governing human experimentation exist, none of these codes are regularly enforced. The codes are useful only in so far as they set standards articulating basic principles of bioethics. At this juncture, their utility as legal tools to force researchers to respect the rights of human subjects is minimal at best. The three most prominent codes - The Nuremberg Code, The Helsinki Declaration and The International Guidelines for Biomedical Research Involving Human Subjects are discussed below.

The Nuremberg Code

The Nuremberg Code created the first internationally acceptable set of legal guidelines regulating research on human beings. It was developed at the end of World War II, after the International Military Tribunal prosecuted twenty-three Nazi scientists and physicians who had designed experiments contemplating the death and dissection of human subjects for war crimes and crimes against humanity. This tribunal, commonly referred to as the Nuremberg Trial, focused the world's attention on the worst possible consequences of unethical and uncontrolled human experimentation.

The guidelines hereinafter referred to as the Nuremberg Code, established ten principles to ensure the moral, ethical, and legal practice of human experimentation. The best known and perhaps the most frequently articulated principle of the Nuremberg Code is the first principle which states that "voluntary consent is absolutely essential." Under the Nuremberg Code, it was deemed impossible for an individual to consent to participate in an experiment without first being fully informed by the researcher about the nature and purpose of the experiment, as well as the risks, hazards and inconveniences to expect. The concept of consent refers to both the subjects' capacity to give consent as well as the researchers' obligation to provide information to their subjects. Consequently, the process of obtaining consent is just as important as the actual giving of consent, and it is the duty and responsibility of each individual who initiates, directs, or engages in an experiment to ensure that the consent of the subject is valid.

Although consent is essential, the Nuremberg Code makes it clear that all of the other nine points of the Nuremberg Code must be satisfied prior to obtaining consent. In essence, the other nine points require that experiments involving human beings should be: (i) designed and based on the results of animal experimentation; (ii) conducted in a manner that avoids unnecessary physical and mental suffering and injury as well as death; and (iii) conducted for the good of society. The Code also requires that only scientifically qualified persons have authorization to conduct experiments on human beings.

The Helsinki Declaration

The World Medical Association enacted the Helsinki Declaration in 1964. Like the Nuremberg Code, the Helsinki Declaration embraces informed consent and the need for experimentation to be conducted by scientifically qualified individuals. It also prescribes that animal and laboratory experiments should precede research on human beings, and it mandates a risk/benefit analysis in which the interest of science should not outweigh the health and safety of the subject. The Declaration, however, has two additional requirements not provided for by the Nuremberg Code. First, the Declaration provides that researchers who fail to fulfill their ethical obligations should be penalized by having their research rejected for publication. Second, it requires an independent ethical committee to provide researchers with comments and guidance on their research protocol. The committee also has the responsibility of verifying that (1) researchers are qualified to conduct the experiment, (2) experiments are properly designed, (3) test subjects have been equitably chosen, (4) privacy of the subjects will be respected, and (5) the potential humanitarian benefits arising from the experiment justify the risk to the individual subjects. The concept of the independent ethical committee represents a significant advancement over the Nuremberg Code because it alleviates the need for investigators to rely solely on their own consciences to guide them in determining whether research is in compliance with basic ethical standards.

Both the ethical review committees and the provision regarding the rejection for publication as a penalty for conducting unethical experiments creates a system of checks and balances that is not present in the Nuremberg Code. The provisions are an attempt at not only setting ethical standards but an attempt to establish a mechanism for monitoring and enforcing ethical requirements in human experimentation.

The International Ethical Guidelines for Biomedical Research Involving Human Subjects

Besides the Nuremberg Code and the Helsinki Declaration, there is one other international ethics document that provides ethical guidance to medical professionals conducting human research. In 1982, the Counsel for International Organizations of Medical Sciences (CIOMS), in collaboration with the World Health Organization (WHO), released the Proposed International Ethical Guidelines for Biomedical Research Involving Human Subjects (Guidelines). These proposed guidelines, based on the 1975 version of the Helsinki Declaration, were offered to countries as a model for national standards.

The Guidelines stressed the need for informed consent, special protection for vulnerable populations, equitable distribution of burdens and benefits associated with research, and the need for independent ethical review committees. The Guidelines were also designed to provide strategies on how to effectively apply the principles of the Helsinki Declaration, particularly in developing countries. The final version of the Guidelines, published in 1991, constituted the most extensive treatment of issues related to human experimentation. Unlike the Declaration and the Code, the Guidelines provide that subjects involved in medical research who suffer injury as a result of their participation in an experiment are entitled to financial compensation for any temporary or permanent disability.

Another remarkable aspect of the Guidelines is that it is the first document to address issues arising from the internationalization of scientific research. In this regard, there are provisions in the Guidelines that specifically address research in developing communities. For example, Guideline 8 requires that research subjects from developing communities not be used in research that could be carried out reasonably well with subjects from developed communities. It attempts to prevent the exploitation of socially and economically disadvantaged communities in developed countries as well.

Guideline 15 addresses externally sponsored research, defined as "research undertaken in a host country that is sponsored, financed, and sometimes wholly or partly carried out by an external or international or national agency with the collaboration or agreement of the appropriate authorities... of the host country." It requires that all externally funded research must meet not only the ethical standards of the host country, but also the ethical standards of the initiating country.

These Guidelines served as the inspiration for more than fifty-five countries that adopted legislation or enacted other measures to regulate human experimentation between 1980 and 1992.

PROBLEMS WITH NUREMBERG/HELSINKI/CIOMS

The Nuremberg Code, the Helsinki Declaration and the International Ethical Guidelines for Biomedical Research Involving Human Subjects are all based on moral or ethical values rather than legal mandates. Although it may be argued that each document has some degree of influence over the conduct of researchers, ultimately these regulations create ethical duties that are only advisory in nature. Moreover, the Guidelines are clearly not intended to be legally binding and must be voluntarily enacted by national legislatures or adopted by a court of law in order to be enforceable.

Although many countries have adopted enforceable legislation modeled after the Guidelines, the Nuremberg Code, or the Helsinki Declaration, each country is free to adopt whatever standards it desires. Some countries have very detailed regulations, while others have very lenient standards or no standards at all. This lack of uniformity, combined with a general lack of enforcement, allows unethical research to be conducted with impunity. Despite the availability of both civil and criminal sanctions for unethical experimentation, there has never been a reported criminal case citing the Nuremberg Code.

Furthermore, even though the Code became part of international customary or common law, and could technically be used as the basis for both civil and criminal cases, a review of the case law in the United States indicates that there are very few American court decisions involving human experimentation in which either the Nuremberg Code or the Helsinki Declaration has ever been cited. In fact, it took twenty-five years after the Code was promulgated for a United States court to use the Nuremberg Code as guidance in a decision. The United States Supreme Court has mentioned the Nuremberg Code in only one dissent. Similarly, there are no reported cases from any international court or human rights agency which cite to the Helsinki Declaration or the Nuremberg Code.

This lack of reliance on the Nuremberg Code and the Helsinki Declaration may be due to the fact that often people injured as a result of human experimentation simply do not have the economic resources to pursue legal remedies. Some may not even know that pursuing a legal remedy is an option. Many individuals who do choose to pursue their legal rights may base their claims on local tort theories of battery, intentional infliction of emotional distress, medical malpractice or negligence, rather than on international law.

Although the failure to apply, monitor and enforce the terms of the codes undermines the significance of these ethical guidelines which purport to regulate human research, these codes do provide significant evidence of international agreement on medical experimentation. Thus, the codes provide an ethical framework for questioning the appropriateness of human experimentation. A detailed examination and analysis of how the provisions of the Nuremberg Code, the Helsinki Declaration and the Guidelines apply to the quinacrine campaign is beyond the scope.

QUINACRINE: A BIOETHICAL ANALYSIS

The Nuremberg Code, the Helsinki Declaration and the International Ethical Guidelines for Biomedical Research Involving Human Subjects all place great emphasis on the principles of beneficence, distributive justice, and autonomy. In bioethical analysis, all three of these principles are important to resolving the ethical problems presented by human experimentation. In this section, these three principles will be used to examine the questions raised by the quinacrine campaign.

Beneficence/Non-malificence

Beneficence and non-maleficence refer to the ethical obligation to maximize benefits and to minimize harms and wrongs. These principles require that the risks of research must be reasonable in light of the expected benefits, that the research design must be sound, and that the investigators must be competent both to conduct the research and to safeguard the welfare of the research subjects.

To begin this analysis, it is necessary to point out that many of the quinacrine sterilizations that have already been performed were done without regard to an established research agenda. Mumford and Kessel believe that quinacrine is not a "new drug," and that its safety has already been established. Therefore, they often failed to conduct themselves as if they were involved in experimental research on human beings. From their perspective, quinacrine had been used to treat malaria and other diseases for over fifty years without any serious side effects. They therefore concluded that quinacrine sterilizations would also be safe and effective.

No consideration was given to the possibility that quinacrine administered intrauterinely for sterilization purposes would most likely have a different effect on one's body and overall health than quinacrine administered orally as a prophylactic for disease. No consideration was given to the fact that quinacrine administered intrauterinely (as opposed to orally) was being used as a schlerosing agent to create scar tissue in a woman's reproductive tract. Despite this obvious difference, Mumford and Kessel claim that quinacrine is "an approved drug in virtually every country of the world" and that the sterilizations are not experimental because they are a legitimate "off label" use of the drug.

By removing quinacrine from the "experimental" category, the doctors believe that they are free to ignore all guidelines governing human experimentation. Consequently, many of the women who have been subjected to quinacrine sterilizations are not being monitored for either long-term or short-term effects, are not being provided with any type of follow up care, and are not being informed that there are potential unknown risks associated with quinacrine sterilizations. In essence, these women are not given the same consideration that is normally given to human subjects participating in medical experiments.

In those cases where women are clearly being treated as if they are "subjects" of a medical study, there is a lack of uniformity in the manner in which the research is conducted. For example, in many instances, the dose of quinacrine administered from woman to woman varied. In other cases, the skill of the health worker performing the sterilizations also varied. Even the informed consent protocol varied from site to site, if it existed at all. In a document published by Mumford and Kessel, they state:

Our decades of experience in working in countries around the world have led us to recognize that our form and our view of informed consent is not always applicable everywhere. We have learned that we must rely on the judgment of our collaborators to decide what is best for their patients.

One interpretation of this statement is that Mumford and Kessel and the clinicians whom they have enlisted to assist them in performing quinacrine sterilizations do not share a common understanding of informed consent. On the other hand, the statement may also be interpreted to mean that in certain circumstances, doctors using quinacrine do not deem informed consent necessary. The lack of informed consent, combined with unreliable research design, and inadequate follow-up in the quinacrine research trials, make it highly unlikely that the results of this "research" will be valid. Without valid results, research utilizing human subjects is not only valueless but probably unethical as well.

To obtain a better understanding of the bioethical questions raised by the quinacrine campaign, however, it is helpful to more closely examine the motivations and alleged benefits of quinacrine sterilizations.

What are the potential benefits of quinacrine sterilization?

Mumford and Kessel claim that they are promoting quinacrine in order to decrease the world's population rate. They claim that since women in developing countries have a high risk of dying from childbirth, sterilization will prolong their lives. They argue that the more sterilizations there are in developing countries, the less maternal mortality there will be. Ultimately, Mumford and Kessel claim that this will benefit not only women of childbearing age but society as a whole. They reason that the more sterilized women there are in developing countries, the fewer children there will be to feed and concomitantly the fewer people there will be to populate the earth - which in Mumford's opinion is a matter of survival. Mumford warns that "the world's population is growing too fast... and no one is doing enough to stop it." He states that if population rates continue to rise, "in time, all nations will be overrun by violent masses." Both Mumford and Kessel have been quoted as stating that chemical sterilization will play a very important role in maintaining peace and security through out the world.

This sentiment connecting national security to the need for population control is not new. In fact, twenty-five years ago, the Central Intelligence Agency, the Agency International Development, and the United States' Departments of State, Defense, and Agriculture produced confidential National Security Study Memorandum 2000 in which the United States government supported population control as a way to stem radical dissent and protect U.S. access to strategic minerals in developing countries. More recently, top State Department officials have indicated they believe overpopulation was a major cause of political strife in Haiti, Rwanda, and Chiapas, Mexico. Similarly, in 1996, the White House announced in the preface to its National Security Strategy report that "large-scale environmental degradation, exacerbated by rapid population growth, threatens to undermine political stability in many countries and regions." One year later, the Rockefeller Foundation embraced this notion and explained the conflict as follows:

Resource scarcities, often exacerbated by population growth, undermine the quality of life, confidence in government, and threaten to destabilize many parts of the globe.... Once a resource becomes scarce, a society's "haves" often seize control of it, leaving an even smaller share for the "have nots." Since population growth rates are highest among the have-nots, this means that an even larger number of people are competing for a smaller share of resources - and violent conflict is often the result.

This alleged nexus between population, violence and political instability in developing countries has spawned a movement that preaches fear and hatred of people from developing countries. Its most recent manifestation is the coalition-building which is occurring between anti-immigration groups, population control groups and environmental organizations. Their shared agenda is a dangerous resentment of immigrants as well as a targeting of immigrant women's fertility. It is at this crossroad that Mumford and Kessel appear. Mumford, in particular, has been very open in espousing his concern for controlling immigration into the United States. He stated:

Immigration is much too high. We have 1.2 million legal immigrants annually and who knows how many illegal.... Every environmental indicator in America is in decline, so immigration already is affecting our quality of life.... This overpopulation bomb is going to drive terrorism in the United States.

Mumford has also stated on film that: "If we don't control our borders, we will certainly become a Third World country. I mean, more than a billion people would like to emigrate here today." Comments such as these, in addition to Mumford's membership in several anti-immigration groups, have lead many people to believe that the motivation behind the quinacrine sterilization campaign is to reduce the number of poor uneducated immigrants to the United States. This belief is also fueled by the fact that Mumford and Kessel's quinacrine campaign is primarily funded by donors who are also avid anti-immigration sponsors.

In 1998, Alix Freedman of the Wall Street Journal reported that the most dedicated fundraisers for the quinacrine sterilization campaign were Donald Collins and Sally Epstein, a couple from Washington D.C., who are both on the board of the Federation for American Immigration Reform (FAIR). This organization advocates for a sharp reduction in immigration to the United States. Also among Mumford and Kessel's contributors are the Scaife Family Foundation (contributing $160,000 to the quinacrine sterilization campaign since 1994) and the Leland Fikes Foundation, both of which are linked to FAIR. Both of these organizations espouse the belief that the United States must limit immigration or be "overwhelmed with immigrants who will turn this nation into another third world country."

In essence, Mumford and Kessel appear to be driven by three incentives in their sterilization crusade: (1) the need to reduce maternal mortality in developing countries in order to save women's lives; (2) the desire to control or reduce the population in Third World countries in order to secure world peace; and (3) the need to prevent immigrants from flooding United States borders in order to prevent chaos and destruction. From Mumford and Kessel's perspective, all three of these incentives are based on their desire to make the world a better place and to "do good."

Assuming for the sake of argument that Mumford and Kessel really are motivated by a desire to "do good," we must now determine how effective the quinacrine experiment is at achieving its allegedly "beneficent" goals. This is one of the key questions in bioethical analysis.

How Effective is Quinacrine at Achieving its Goals ?

1. Chemical sterilization will reduce maternal mortality

In terms of a risk/benefit analysis for quinacrine sterilization, Kessel states:

> A simple guide to determining benefits is the estimate for rural areas of South countries that each sterilization prevents two births. If maternal mortality is, say 3.8 per 1,000 live births as estimated for Vietnam, then each 1,000 sterilizations done by a new method such as quinacrine pellets will prevent 7.6 maternal deaths. No one has suggested that the method could kill that number of women.

In making this statement, Kessel is trying to reinforce the notion that quinacrine sterilizations are good because they will reduce maternal mortality and save lives. Kessel's analysis regarding the relationship between sterilization and maternal mortality, however, is fatally flawed. The problem is that the analysis assumes that all women at risk of maternal death in developing countries - *i.e.* pregnant women - do not want to be pregnant and that they want to be sterilized. His analysis fails to account for the many women who consciously choose to be pregnant. For these women, sterilization is not a desired option. His analysis also ignores the many women who, although they seek to prevent pregnancy, would deliberately reject sterilization as an acceptable form of contraception and instead choose to use other less invasive forms of contraceptives that are not permanent.

Several of these other forms of contraceptives are also arguably more beneficial than quinacrine sterilizations because they have a higher effectiveness rate in preventing pregnancy and/or providing protection against HIV. Use of condoms, for example, would promote male responsibility for sexual conduct, in addition to providing protection against HIV. Other contraceptive alternatives which may be more effective at preventing pregnancy include the female condom, the pill, the IUD, the diaphragm used with spermicide, Norplant, and Depo-provera. Since there are so many other alternatives to prevent pregnancy besides quinacrine, it is simply scientifically inaccurate to juxtapose the risks of maternity with the benefits of quinacrine sterilization. As Marge Berer has pointed out, risks and benefits of quinacrine sterilization are appropriately compared only with those of other sterilization methods. When, however, quinacrine is compared to surgical sterilization, it does not fare particularly well: quinacrine has a higher failure rate and presents unknown risks to fetuses and infants who are conceived post-sterilization.

Although in developing countries, complications in childbirth literally kill hundreds of thousands of poor women every year and pregnancy-related deaths desperately need to be reduced, it is not true that quinacrine sterilizations are the most beneficial way of addressing this public health problem. Studies indicate that maternal mortality is caused by unhealthy lifestyles, poor nutrition, a lack of access to health care in general and less access to prenatal care specifically. Prescriptions to reduce maternal mortality should therefore address at least one of the root causes of the problem. Quinacrine sterilization, however, do not address any of these root causes. This casts significant doubt on Mumford and Kessel's claim that quinacrine will benefit women who are at risk of maternal death.

2. Chemical sterilization will limit immigration to the United States

According to Mumford and Kessel, reducing maternal mortality is not the only benefit of quinacrine sterilization. According to them, chemical sterilization will also (a) reduce third world populations thereby decreasing political chaos and promoting world peace, and (b) limit immigration to the United States thereby preventing further terrorism in and destruction of this country. The problem with these objectives is that they articulate a political rather than a medical objective.

If the doctors involved in this experiment actually attempt to achieve these political objectives, there is a great risk that the autonomy of the women subjected to quinacrine sterilizations will be severely curtailed. The doctors, when faced with the choice of focusing on what the women need or focusing on the so called "needs" of society, will be placed in an untenable position. They will need to weigh the importance of their own political objectives against the health interests of the women to whom they are providing services.

In this scenario, women in developing countries are viewed as a means rather than an end in themselves. Kantian principles of ethics maintain that "we should treat others as autonomous ends and never as means to our own ends" because people should be valued in and of themselves. In the quinacrine campaign, women are being treated as a means to achieve lower third world population rates, not because it is in the best interest of the women to have fewer children, but because it will allegedly benefit the world and "American culture." This type of philosophy subjugates women's interests to a political agenda which is steeped in xenophobia, racism, and classism.

This desire to limit the population of a certain segment of society is hauntingly similar to traditional eugenics philosophy which calls for the elimination of those who are deemed to be "undesirable" or "unfit" individuals. The political objectives of the proponents of quinacrine sterilization make it clear that the chemical sterilization campaign is not designed to save lives by decreasing the rate of maternal mortality. Instead it is designed to prevent the creation of new lives by eliminating the capacity of certain women to reproduce.

Distributive Justice

The evidence clearly establishes that throughout the ages and down to the present, the people used as unknowing or unwilling subjects of experimentation are the poor; the racially or nationally oppressed; the imprisoned or the institutionalized; the very young or the very aged; and women more often than men.

Generally speaking, distributive justice refers to the ethical obligation to treat each person fairly or in accordance with what is morally right. More specifically, it requires the equitable distribution of both the burdens and the benefits of participation in research. This principle dictates that no one group - socio-economic, gender, racial, ethnic, or geographic - should bear the burden or be denied the benefits of research. Thus, beneficial research should not be offered only to favored individuals. Nor should "undesirable" or "disadvantaged" persons be the only ones selected for risky research.

In terms of quinacrine, it is clear that most if not all of the women subjected to quinacrine sterilizations are disadvantaged: they are low income rural women with very little education living in developing countries. It is also clear that quinacrine research may be categorized as "risky" since quinacrine has not been tested adequately on animals and nothing is known about (a) its long term side effects, (b) its potential to cause cancer, or (c) the potential harm that fetuses exposed to quinacrine and infants exposed to quinacrine through breast milk will experience. Given these facts, we must question why women in developing countries are the sole target for the quinacrine sterilization campaign.

Socially and economically disadvantaged people have historically been disproportionately represented as subjects of human experimentation. It is no secret that groups such as prisoners, institutionalized persons, and military personnel, in addition to historically disadvantaged groups, such as African Americans in the United States, have been exploited by medical researchers. Like all of these groups, women in developing countries are more easily coerced and manipulated into participation in human experimentation by virtue of their lack of economic, political, and social status.

This lack of status often correlates with illiteracy, a reluctance to question those of "greater" status and an inability to access legal or governmental agencies that are capable of providing recourse for harm suffered. These conditions make the economically and socially disadvantaged prime candidates for exploitation in human experimentation. For this reason, close scrutiny of the quinacrine campaign is even more important.

To justify their decision to focus the distribution of quinacrine in developing countries, Kessel and his associates argue that using a riskier sterilization method is justified because women's lives in developing countries are more at risk not only in pregnancy but in general. One of Mumford and Kessel's medical associates in Bangladesh framed the issue as follows: "e have a mortality rate of forty to forty-five for women. These women are going to die anyway be it from malaria, diarrhea or some form of cancer. So, if there are long term complications with quinacrine it does not matter." Another Mumford/Kessel associate in Bangladesh, gynecologist Naseem Rahman, stated the following:

The developed world's cautious standards of medical ethics and safety have no place in the lives of women for who repeated pregnancies bring nothing but deprivation and danger.... As it is, they're going to die, so what do the long-term complications of quinacrine matter?

If this simple equation is correct - higher risk in pregnancy justifies higher risk in contraceptive method - Kessel and his cohorts would have to conclude that it is also appropriate for African-American women to be subjected to greater contraceptive risks than white women in the United States because African-American women are four times more likely to die from pregnancy-related complications than white women. Using this rationale, it would also be logical to conclude that it is appropriate for poor women in general to be subjected to greater contraceptive risk than wealthy women because poor women are at greater risk in pregnancy than wealthier women. The problem with these arguments is that they promote a social theory that deems the lives and health of certain individuals to be more important and worthy of protection than others.

Those who have resources and access to health care are worthy of all that is good including good health. Those who are poor in resources and health, on the other hand, are not worthy and are therefore deemed to be suitable for all sorts of health risks.

Categorizing human subjects as "less worthy" allows the researchers to construct psychological and emotional space between themselves and their subjects. Since most researchers maintain a status in society which affirms their "worthiness," they begin to view the human subject as something "other" than them. Once the subject is labeled "other," it is easier for the researcher to perceive the human subject as being less emotional (or simply unemotional) less capable of experiencing pain; and ultimately less valuable. Being less worthy or valuable, the well-being of the socially and economically disadvantaged is deemed to be inconsequential, and concomitantly, their participation in experimentation that involves unknown health risks becomes acceptable.

Thus, in terms of quinacrine, women in developing countries are deemed to be expendable because they will either die from malnutrition, malaria, some form of cancer or from pregnancy. Putting these women at risk is therefore viewed to be a relative concept in which poor health or health complications are viewed as simple nuisances which are always preferable to death. The rationale of the researchers then becomes - "you might not be healthy, but you won't be pregnant and dead." Options for women in developing nations do not include living a healthier life or maintaining a healthy pregnancy. Thus, Mumford and Kessel do not advocate strategies to make pregnancy safer for these women but instead call for the elimination of their ability to become pregnant. Rather than improve the health care systems that are failing to provide safe maternal options, these social strategists call for the alteration of women's bodies. From their perspective, the problem is not the system, it is the women themselves.

Kessel and Mumford do not offer any persuasive reason why quinacrine is disproportionately offered to women in developing countries. The alleged potential benefits of quinacrine do not appear to outweigh the harm to women's bodies, emotions and their integrity. This inequitable distribution of burdens violates the basic principle of justice.

AUTONOMY

The principle of autonomy primarily focuses on the need to respect an individual's capacity for self-determination. Thus, individuals who are capable of deliberating about their personal goals must be treated with respect. Respect for the autonomy of a human subject can be demonstrated by (a) providing information to human subjects about the nature of their research; (b) by informing them that there may be unknown risks associated with the process; (c) by revealing all known risks of injury; and (d) by discussing alternative treatments. It is only after all the risks and the alternative treatments have been explained in simple language capable of being understood by the individual that an individual can consent to participation in an experiment. In addition, the process of obtaining consent must be free of deception and coercion. These requirements are commonly referred to as the principles of informed consent. If a potential research subject has not been adequately informed, she cannot freely decide, in accordance with her own values, whether or not to participate in experimentation. Thus, if decision making is inhibited by any actions of the researchers, the individual's self-determination has not been respected.

In the quinacrine controversy, it has been reported that many of the women who were sterilized did not know what was happening to them. For example, in 1989, after Vietnam's family planning program had performed more than thirty thousand quinacrine sterilizations, it was reported that women working at the Hoa Binh Rubber Plantation were involuntarily sterilized. According to Mumford, approximately one hundred and seven Vietnamese women employed by this privately-owned rubber plantation were sterilized without knowing or understanding that they were being permanently sterilized. One of these women, Nguyen Thi, reported that on March 10, 1993, she went to the plantation health clinic, where she was told that she would receive a routine gynecological examination. Instead, the clinic's doctor removed her IUD and performed quinacrine sterilization.

Although most of the details about the Vietnam sterilizations remain buried, a senior employee of the rubber plantation has stated that the doctor who performed the sterilizations did so to enhance his career by helping enforce Vietnam's two-child policy. However, the doctor, who was not fired, insists he sterilized the women in accordance with orders from plantation officials. No comment has been made by the Hoa Binh Rubber Plantation regarding this matter. Other people speculate that the managers at the plantation orchestrated the campaign to keep productivity high. As a result of intense pressure from the World Health Organization, the quinacrine sterilization program in Vietnam was abandoned.

Unfortunately, quinacrine sterilization abuse in Vietnam was not an isolated incident. In Pakistan, Dr. Bashir of the Faisalabad Mother and Child Welfare Association reported sterilizing two thousand one hundred women in 1990 alone. An independent nurse-practitioner who went to Faisalabad in 1993 to observe Dr. Bashir's clinical work reported that some of Bashir's patients were recruited at "street camps" and were "given little information or time to fully understand and think about the implications of this type of procedure." The nurse-practitioner reported that insertions were conducted by health workers who were unable to provide essential information regarding quinacrine due to their limited clinical skills. As for follow-up of clients who were sterilized, the nurse stated: "The patient is told to return if she has any problems. Those who do not return are assumed to have no problems."

Similar problems regarding the failure to adequately inform women about the quinacrine procedure and the failure to provide follow-up care arose in India as well. In a documentary film entitled The Yellow Haze, produced in 1997 by students of the Jamia Millia University in India, thirty-three women who received quinacrine sterilizations were interviewed. In one of the interviews, Indu Das, a twenty-seven year old mother of three reported that in 1995 when she sought contraceptive counseling from her doctor, he informed her that quinacrine could prevent childbirth for approximately ten to fifteen years. Das then signed, but did not read, an "informed consent" form. She underwent one quinacrine procedure in which one dose of seven pellets of quinacrine (rather than the two doses of quinacrine that are required) was inserted through her uterus. Immediately after this procedure, Indu experienced severe bleeding. Two years later, she became pregnant and had to have an abortion.

If it were not for the Yellow Haze documentary, this woman's story would never have been told since the doctor who performed the sterilization made no report of the incident. Other women interviewed in this documentary also indicated that they, like Indu Das, were not told of the risks associated with quinacrine. These women reported that they suffered side effects, including swelling of the feet, severe abdominal pain and depression.

Following the release of The Yellow Haze documentary, the All India Democratic Women's Association and faculty members of the Center for Community Health at Jawaharlal Nehru University filed a lawsuit claiming that thirty thousand Indian women had been involuntarily subjected to quinacrine sterilizations without their knowledge or consent. Shortly thereafter, the Indian government banned the import, manufacturing, sale, and distribution of quinacrine for use as a sterilizing agent. Violators of the ban were subject to imprisonment for up to three years or a fine of up to Rs. 5,000 or both.

All of these stories illustrate that deception and/or coercion were used as part of the process in recruiting women to be chemically sterilized. These are clear examples of experimentation that lack respect for autonomy. There also appear to be more subtle ways in which women's autonomy in this chemical sterilization experiment may not have been respected. For example, it is doubtful that the doctors involved in this experiment have ever bothered to inform the women of the potential health risks associated with quinacrine. One need only look at Mumford's response to a Wall Street Journal chapter to come to this conclusion.

In a letter to the Journal, Mumford states that he "firmly rejects the idea that there are any serious scientific concerns that quinacrine may cause cancer." He also states rather defensively and unpersuasively that it is simply "a lie" that the safety and effectiveness of quinacrine sterilizations have not been resolved. He offers no evidence that these issues have been resolved (perhaps because there is no evidence to support a claim that quinacrine sterilizations are safe and effective). Mumford simply states that he believes "quinacrine sterilizations offer women worldwide a safe, sure, non-surgical and inexpensive way to end childbearing." He also claims that the concerns regarding carcinogenicity of quinacrine are the product of a "feminist conspiracy." This assertion is mind-boggling, particularly in light of the fact that well respected, non-feminist health organizations like the FDA, the WHO, the AVSC, FHI, and Planned Parenthood have all stated that they have serious concerns regarding quinacrine's safety and potential for causing cancer. Statements such as these indicate that Mumford may not be capable of making a fair or balanced presentation of the facts associated with quinacrine's side effects.

Kessel's and Mumford's writings, as well as the writings of the doctors associated with them, downplay the significance of the potential side effects associated with quinacrine. None of the published medical reports on quinacrine mention that quinacrine slurries caused the death of three women. In fact, Kessel brags that over "100,000 procedures have been performed in twenty countries without a case fatality." Kessel criticizes those who mention these deaths because he claims that they were caused by quinacrine "slurries," not quinacrine pellets, which he claims is an entirely different method of sterilization. Nonetheless, when the tables are turned and Mumford attempts to prove that quinacrine is "safe," he makes two major claims: (1) that there are 20,000 published scientific papers on quinacrine, and (2) there are one hundred million people who have used this drug without harm. The 100,000,000 people and the 20,000 scientific papers he refers to pertain not to women who have been sterilized with quinacrine but people who were using quinacrine to treat malaria. How Mumford can be upset by the comparison of one form of quinacrine sterilizations to another form of quinacrine sterilization but not be bothered by his own comparison of quinacrine sterilizations to use of quinacrine for non-sterilization purposes is a glaring example of hypocrisy and perhaps even deception.

Kessel has stated that all quinacrine side effects "are transient and easily treated." Although it is true that most of the side effects are not necessarily life-threatening, some could in fact be fatal. For example, perforation of the uterus and ectopic pregnancies are both potentially fatal conditions in areas where there are no emergency medical facilities. Furthermore, many other side effects are not accurately described as "transient or easily treated." For example, women who become pregnant due to an incomplete blockage of the fallopian tubes subsequent to quinacrine sterilization have given birth to children with serious disabilities. There is at least one reported case of anencephaly, being born without a brain, and another reported case of hydrocephaly.

Due to the fact that no serious follow-up studies have been completed, it is impossible to determine the exact nature and severity of the side effects. As the FDA has pointed out:

Currently available information on the safety, efficacy and clinical experience with quinacrine sterilization is based upon clinical trials which lack appropriate study design, are poorly controlled, have incomplete follow- up on study participants and are not comparable due to differences in formulation, dose, dosing regimen and adjuvant therapies used.

Based on this history, it is therefore doubtful that Mumford and his colleagues (those who were trained by him) would be able to clearly articulate the side effects and risks associated with quinacrine in a manner that would be consistent with the notion of informed consent. The diminishment of the significance of side effects and the lack of concern about the potential carcinogencity of quinacrine by the doctors involved in this experiment, in combination with willingness to conduct involuntary quinacrine sterilizations indicate that respect for the principle of autonomy is clearly lacking.

Even if autonomy were respected by obtaining informed consent from the women to be sterilized, the experiment would still be unethical. As Robert Burt points out in connection with the Nazi experiments, "the consent of the experimental subjects would not have justified the experiments" because obtaining consent in clinical research is not the only requirement for ethical validity. The principles of beneficence/non-maleficence and distributive justice must also be considered. In the case of quinacrine, none of the principles of bioethics have been sufficiently respected.

CONCLUSION

In November 2000, the FDA approved a clinical trial of quinacrine to be conducted by Dr. Jack Lippes at the Children's Hospital of Buffalo, in Buffalo, New York. This trial will involve ten women as human subjects. Although FDA clinical trials will provide an environment more conducive to respecting women's rights to obtain information and follow-up care, it is a double-edged sword. With United States backed quinacrine research, the research previously conducted in developing countries will be buried under this new found FDA "legitimacy." All of the questionable studies that were done will be overshadowed by the FDA approved experiments. Thus, the women in developing countries who were ill-informed and ill-treated will be forgotten and swept under the proverbial rug.

In addition to the amnesia regarding prior clinical trials, the introduction of quinacrine in the United States raises several other issues and concerns. How and to whom will quinacrine be marketed in the United States? Will there be the same type of population control politics at work? What assurances will there be that women "selected" for quinacrine sterilizations will have the opportunity to exercise their right to informed consent? Given the history of reproductive technology, as well as the stated objective of advancing quinacrine sterilizations, it is likely that low-income women will be the target of the quinacrine campaign in the United States. As one quinacrine advocate has stated, "the major advantage of quinacrine sterilizations in the USA and elsewhere is its increased access for women who cannot afford surgical sterilization." What this tells us is that women with little or no resources are prime candidates for quinacrine sterilizations. Like women in developing countries, women in the developed world with little or no resources are considered to be "expendable." They are not targeted as prime candidates because they volunteer for this position, nor because they have a demonstrated need for chemical sterilization. They are prime candidates for sterilization because they are thought to be the source of the world's population "problem." This desire to fulfill the political objective of controlling the population has led doctors involved in the quinacrine campaign to completely ignore the well-established principle that no one should be subjected to experimentation without their consent. This lack of respect for autonomy is reprehensible but not new.

Historically, sterilization has been abused in low income and politically powerless communities. Consequently, when sterilization is promoted as a means of preventing pregnancy, suspicion and scrutiny are warranted. And when a sterilization method such as quinacrine is being promoted as a weapon in the womb of women in developing countries, heightened scrutiny and suspicion are warranted. Should we allow quinacrine sterilizations to be advanced and perfected when there is clear evidence that this method has already been used to abuse the rights of women?

The Helsinki Declaration states that the "potential benefits, hazards, and discomfort of a new method should be weighed against the advantages of the best current diagnostic and therapeutic methods." Presently, there are several other options available for preventing pregnancy that is safer than quinacrine. There are also several other methods of preventing pregnancy currently under development, which would place a more equitable burden on both men and women. These forms of contraception may be more deserving of scientific resources than quinacrine sterilizations.

Although many people argue that scientific research is necessary to advance our knowledge as a society, we must keep in mind that not all advances in science are in the best interest of humanity. Quinacrine, in the best case scenario, may prevent unwanted pregnancies, but it does so without guarantees of protection against sexually transmitted diseases and with a failure rate that exceeds other contraceptives currently available. Although a pregnancy is not always desirable, it is not a disease. It does not beg for a cure at the cost of human dignity, autonomy, or justice. In biomedical research considerations related to the well-being of the human subject should take precedence over the interests of science and society.

So far, there is no convincing evidence that the benefits of quinacrine research outweigh the risks to women or fetuses. Nor is there any evidence that women anywhere in the world are in need of chemical sterilizations as an option for preventing pregnancy. The fact that the doctors involved in this research claim that quinacrine sterilizations are safe and effective when no evidence exists to support this claim is outrageous and particularly alarming in light of the serious questions regarding quinacrine's mutagencity, carcinogenicity, and effectiveness at preventing pregnancy that have been raised by several entities, including the World Health Organization. Quinacrine was presumed to be safe and then introduced outside of the avenues for "mainstream research." This lack of precedent for declaring a medical procedure to be "safe" is testimony to the fact that the researchers involved in this campaign do not care about the well-being of the women who serve as their human subjects.

In spite of this, the doctors/researchers involved in this chemical sterilization campaign not only continue to publish their selected "findings," but they continue to have access to large audiences of doctors and public health officials. Their access to publications as well as well-respected audiences should be denied until retrospective studies of women who were already treated with quinacrine are completed. This would be consistent with the provisions of the Helsinki Declaration.

Although medical experiments conducted on an international basis are not governed by any legally binding provisions that are actively enforced, health professionals and legal activists can insist that researchers respect the bioethical principles consistent with the Nuremberg Code, the Helsinki Declaration, and the International Ethical Guidelines for Research Involving Human Subjects. Unless we take a closer look at the ethical dimensions of the quinacrine campaign, the devaluation of women's lives in both developing and developed countries will continue. Health professionals and legal activists should emphasize the ethics or lack of ethics involved in the quinacrine campaign in order to set a threshold for what will be considered acceptable objectives and procedures for future experimentation. The history of abuse and lack of justice involved in the quinacrine experiments should not be tolerated or forgotten.

5

The Human Rights of International Black Women in the United States

The onward march of globalization is as much responsible for this reality as is the tradition of migrancy among Caribbean peoples. New imperial powers - transnational corporations, international economic agencies, and the governments that buttress those powers -are increasingly responsible, but not accountable, for the well-being of the millions who move from the South to the North and back again. Transnational corporations move freely from country to country to find low-cost labor and less-restrictive government regulation and encourage migrant laborers to follow.

International and regional trade agreements and the structural-adjustment policies of international aid agencies threaten to destabilize the security of both workers and governments. The economic devastation of the South leads desperate workers to flee to the North, where they provide the agricultural, assembly, and domestic labor that supports northern economies. Many of those laborers then share "the bottom of the well" with the poor people of color and women who make up the hard-core underclass. In a pattern full of ironies and contradictions, those at the top of northern economies then fashion international aid and lending policies that perpetuate the process.

Increasingly, poor women of color from the Global South are among those who attempt to make their way amid the remnants of gutted social-welfare supports at home and abroad. Unable to find adequate wages or other necessities to support themselves and their families, these women follow opportunities to work across geographic borders. In doing so, they cross legal, political, cultural, and economic borders as well. What are the implications of making the passage of Black women back and forth across these "international" boundaries visible? Can legal scholarship fully engage their experiences of the spaces they occupy? How do these Black women escape or resist the centers of power they encounter in their international struggle to survive? Indeed, can legal scholarship contribute to a deeper understanding of the conditions under which they live? Without such an understanding, it will be impossible to develop policies that would help to alleviate those abusive conditions.

Although most Jamaican women identify themselves as Black, they are still regarded as "other" by some Americans, including some African Americans. Conversely, the particularity of their experience is often subsumed under an externally imposed essential definition of "Black." Moreover, while many refugees, migrants, displaced persons, and "voluntary" immigrants are female, the gender-specific aspects of their experiences remain largely invisible.

Such women do not easily fit on one side or the other of the Western and Third World divides associated with the international feminist human rights movement. The specifics of their lives are overlooked when they are treated as universal "women," or their multiple identities as geographic and cultural travelers are essentialized as "alien" or "exotic other."

This Chapter calls for a more explicit engagement of critical race scholarship with feminist international human rights strategies and the expansion of the nascent interaction of critical race feminist approaches with international human rights is essential under current conditions of multiculturalism and globalization. To begin the larger project by raising important issues for further exploration by identifying areas in which the human rights of international Black women slip through the cracks of international human rights law and domestic critical race theory. The failures to focus on international Black women rob legal scholarship of rich veins of material for progressive analysis. That analysis could contribute to the building of stronger coalitions for international social justice.

OVERVIEW OF JAMAICAN MIGRATION TO THE UNITED STATES

Many people think of the migration of West Indians to the United States as part of the influx of "new immigrants" that followed changes in U.S. immigration law in 1965 and again in the mid-1980s. Nevertheless, Afro-creole peoples have been a significant part of Black-American communities for more than a century.

Of course, the islands of the Caribbean, particularly Jamaica, were major trans-shipment points in the infamous Triangular Trade of slaves, sugar, and other "commodities" among Great Britain and the American colonies. The sugar plantations of the Caribbean were important seasoning grounds for kidnapped African peoples-it was there that many were to be prepared for lives as property, whether in mainland American colonies, or in the Caribbean itself. Many were beaten, raped, separated from family and ethnic groups, or killed outright. As in the United States, female slaves in Jamaica worked with male slaves to resist. They organized rebellions, poisoned the meals of slave-owners, and refused to bear children. Some Blacks, known as Maroons, escaped to remote regions in the mountains of Jamaica and engaged in armed resistance.

For many African slaves, their "migration in chains" to the American mainland involved relatively brief stays in the Caribbean. Soon, however, the population of Blacks born in the Caribbean began to grow. A few individual free Blacks, usually male, were able to migrate voluntarily from the

Caribbean to the United States in the eighteenth and nineteenth centuries.

The first significant cohort of West Indian immigrants to the United States arrived in the early twentieth century. Most settled in Harlem, New York, which had become a Mecca where Blacks lived and worked in relative autonomy from the forms of racism prevalent in the South. Migrants from the Caribbean also came to escape harsh conditions. Sociologist Nancy Foner notes a number of historical and modern catalysts for the migration of Jamaicans to the United States:

Since the end of the nineteenth century, there have simply been too many Jamaicans on the island with too few opportunities to earn what they consider a decent living. Small farmers, victims of unequal land distribution patterns, do not have enough land. When Jamaicans look to other or additional ways to make a living (and increasing numbers of young people have left the rural parishes for Kingston in recent years), they are very often disappointed. The big growth industries of the post-World War II period in the nonagricultural sector-bauxite, manufacturing, construction, and tourism-have not created many new jobs Even though most migrants had jobs before they left the island, employment was many times not steady or only part time. And all too frequently, earnings were very low and prospects for advancement dim

Among the early migrants also were Caribbean Americans-particularly those with skilled trades or professions-who believed that the newly constituted critical mass of Blacks in the North would create new work opportunities. Others found Harlem to be a promising site for organizing people around racial and economic justice issues. One scholar summarized the prevailing images of male West Indian immigrants of the period as follows:

Legend has it that the West Indian came to Harlem to "teach, open a church, or start trouble."... The development of left wing organizations among Negroes is largely attributed to him, to the extent that the typical Negro Radical was described as "an overeducated West Indian without a job."

While Black immigrants and native-born Blacks often worked together amicably in Harlem, there were also significant tensions among them. These tensions were fostered by conscious and subconscious efforts of some in native-born and Caribbean-born groups to differentiate themselves from the "other" for cultural, economic, or political reasons.

Female immigrants from the Caribbean arrived in much smaller numbers than men during this period. A few prominent individuals, such as Amy Ashwood Garvey and Amy Jacques Garvey, were active in both pan-Africanist and feminist movements. Most of the working-class women who migrated to the United States, however, did so to rejoin male relatives who had preceded them. Many worked in garment industry sweatshops alongside immigrants from Eastern Europe and Asia. Still, few Caribbean women were able to cross legal and cultural barriers to migration. While there was no deep-rooted cultural barrier to Jamaican women working outside the home, males were still considered the primary breadwinners both in Jamaica and by U.S. immigration authorities. Most Black immigrants were males, who either sought temporary work abroad to support families in the Caribbean, or were permanent immigrants who married Americans or sent for their wives and children after finding stable work.

For many women who remained in the Caribbean, however, the benefits of the emigration of male partners and relatives they hoped for were not forthcoming. Women were left to manage children and households on the sometimes meager remittances male relatives could afford to send; others were abandoned once the relative arrived in the United States.

Caribbean immigration to the United States remained relatively stable and light until the mid-1960s. Only a small number of people per year had been allowed to enter the United States after the McCarran-Walter legislation of 1952. Those Jamaicans who had British passports could migrate more easily to Britain to fill labor shortages in that country after World War II.

By the mid-1960s, there were some 56,000 Caribbean-American immigrants in New York City alone. After 1965, that number rose dramatically due to changes in immigration policy in both the United States and Britain. In Britain, anti-immigrant fervor underpinned laws which severely limited the number of people of color from former British colonies allowed to enter England. In the United States, however, the 1965 Immigration Act removed country-specific limitations on the number of immigrants who could enter the United States from the Americas. Between 1965 and 1974, 156,920 Caribbean immigrants migrated to New York City, 52,620 of whom were Jamaican. By 1980, foreign-born Blacks represented 3.1% of the U.S. Black population and 19.3% of the Blacks in the New York City area. Those numbers rose significantly after 1980, following the declaration of amnesty windows for undocumented immigrants who could then send for close relatives.

Rather than settle in Harlem, many of the new Caribbean immigrants moved to other parts of New York where housing for Blacks became available as a result of the U.S. civil rights movement. They formed communities in Brooklyn and Queens that now sustain large West Indian populations: East Flatbush, Crown Heights, Bedford-Stuyvesant, and Jamaica (Queens). Those who were able to achieve relatively stable middle-class status often moved to literally greener pastures in Long Island communities such as Hempstead and Uniondale.

CONSTRUCTING JAMAICAN WOMEN IMMIGRANTS

Unlike previous Caribbean migrations, women predominated among the post-1965 immigrant groups. The demand for low-wage female labor had increased both in the healthcare industry and in private homes. In the new cohort of immigrants, women often arrived first, and then sent for husbands and children. Like Black women in the United

States, Jamaican women had a long history of work outside their own homes (dating back to slavery) and had participated in whatever limited paid labor opportunities were available in Jamaica.

Since emancipation, Jamaican women have been actively involved in occupations outside the home. Indeed, in the 1970s, women constituted about 40 percent of the labor force, although they suffered more than twice the rate of male unemployment, with female unemployment running as high as 36 percent in 1976.

As of 1996, there were approximately 296,000 Jamaican-born women living in the United States. Of that number, 198,000 are non-citizens. Most working-class Jamaican women immigrants are concentrated in the light manufacturing and service sectors of the paid labor force. According to Foner, "female Jamaican migrants in New York are overwhelmingly concentrated in the lower ranks of nursing and healthcare occupations and in private household work as domestics, childcare workers, and companions or aides to the elderly."

The concentration of Jamaican-American working-class women in these occupations is a result of racial and gender politics in Jamaica, the United States, and the global economy as well as of the reflection of preferences of the women themselves. Changes in U.S. immigration policy in response to the increased demand for low-wage female labor, combined with dismal socio-economic conditions in Jamaica to account for the increasing migration of working-class Jamaican women. For most, the work they found in the United States constituted what Foner calls "industrialized housework".

The wages of Jamaican migrant women are, for various reasons, generally lower than those of men. They are limited in the choice of work due to sexual divisions in the labor market-often confined to menial, low prestige, and poorly paying jobs.... In New York, in fact, many Jamaican women live in private homes as domestic workers where they face arbitrary working conditions, low pay, isolation, and lack of autonomy.

Those with primary responsibility for their own small children must work only part-time, remain unemployed, leave their children in the care of relatives and friends in Jamaica, or find a way to sponsor a female relative with whom they could share childcare responsibilities.

HEALTH INDUSTRY WORKERS

The dominant popular image of Jamaican women immigrants as workers is that of a nurse, nurse's aide, or home health aide. As of 1979, thirty-two percent of Caribbean women in New York City worked as a nurse or nurse's aide. In some inner city hospitals in Brooklyn, Caribbean immigrants comprise an extremely high proportion of the non-physician healthcare staff. Nursing was particularly attractive as a career for those women who could meet the educational requirements. In Jamaica itself, nursing was considered a high status field for women. Some immigrant nurses were recruited from Caribbean nursing schools to satisfy nursing shortages in the United States during the 1970s and 1980s. By the mid to late 1990s, waves of hospital mergers, downsizing and managed care resulted in cutbacks in the number of professional nurses in U.S. hospitals and to corresponding cutbacks in recruitment overseas.

While registered nurses, especially those with advanced degrees, are generally better off financially than most working-class immigrant women, their status may be more precarious than it would seem at first glance. Nursing is a female-dominated profession. Feminist scholars have noted that wage scales, benefits, and working conditions are lower than that of men in comparable professions. Many nurses of color experience gender, racial, and ethnic discrimination in hiring and promotion. Those few who reach senior ranks (with the accompanying improvements in wages and benefits) increasingly experience layoffs related to age discrimination and cost-cutting measures. Many are financially responsible for their children, whether in the United States or in Jamaica, as well as for the well-being of members of their extended family. In the New York City area, Jamaican-American nurses and much lower-paid aides, work in greatest numbers in the hospitals and nursing homes that serve inner-city communities. The patients in many of these institutions are people of color who are poor, elderly, or victims of violence and lack access to preventative health care and appropriate nutrition. The jobs of those who care for them, therefore, are often stressful, dirty, and even physically dangerous.

Home health aides bridge the gap between those who work as nurses or aides in hospitals or nursing homes and those who work in private homes as domestics or nannies. For better or worse, in recent years home health care has increasingly been emphasized. Changes in national health programs such as Medicaid and Medicare have encouraged this shift. Further, despite the increasing participation of middle-class women in the non-household labor force, they are still expected to take primary responsibility for elderly relatives and children. This dilemma increased demand for low-wage labor in the home. These fundamental shifts have led to the mushrooming of home healthcare agencies. The agencies employ low-wage workers, the vast majority of whom are women immigrants from the Caribbean and Latin America. The women care for elderly patients and others who have short or long term illnesses, assisting them with personal care, cooking, cleaning, and visit to doctors. Like other forms of domestic work, the quality of working conditions can vary enormously. The work requires long hours as well as physical strength. Because of the rapidity of growth in home healthcare, the low overhead required to open an agency, and relatively little regulatory oversight, the industry has been ripe for incidents of patient-abuse and exploitation of workers.

NANNIES AND DOMESTIC WORKERS

Another well-known image of working-class Jamaican women immigrants is as household workers and "nannies." According to U.S. Census data, of the approximately 64,000 Caribbean-American women who were employed in 1979 in New York City, 7,460 were classified as "servant, cleaner, maids or housekeepers." The current number of domestic workers from the Caribbean in New York City is probably much higher because many such workers are undocumented or women who overstay tourist visas.

As was the case in healthcare, female immigrants filled the need for childcare in middle-class American homes. As a result of the feminist movements of the 1960s and 1970s, middle-class white women were encouraged to work outside the home, but little structural provision was made for the home- based tasks that they had traditionally performed (or which African-American, Asian-American, Latina or Irish-American working-class women had performed for the wealthy). In addition, changes in the U.S. economy made it necessary for many families to generate a dual income in order to maintain a middle-class standard of living. Yet middle-class women were still expected to be responsible for cooking, cleaning, childcare, and elder care tasks.

These economic and social pressures are reflected in U.S. immigration law, which has effectively encouraged the migration of undocumented, "unskilled" women. The law allows employers to hire undocumented workers if they attest that no documented workers or U.S. citizens can be found to fill the job "at the prevailing wage." In 1985, this "was considered to be $200 for a forty-four hour work week." Employers can then sponsor an undocumented worker in her application for a green card and permanent resident status. In the New York area, this system has usually resulted in the employment of women who enter the United States on tourist visas and stay beyond the expiration of their visas to work as domestics or childcare workers.

Recent reports indicate that the waiting period for transition to permanent status under this method has risen from about two years in the early 1990s to current estimates of ten to twenty years. The opportunities for exploitation of these women are numerous, ranging from underpayment of agreed-upon wages and the refusal of time off, to physical abuse or rape. In addition, many women suffer heart-rending separations from their children and other family members.

In some cases, their own children may no longer be minors by the time their mothers see them again. In addition, the prospect of working for only one family has diminished. The waiting period for legalization has grown longer than the time that the original employing family would need childcare. If the women return to their home islands, even for brief periods, they may have to begin the legalization waiting period all over again, or they may risk deportation upon their return to the United States.

INTERNATIONAL STRATEGIES OF SURVIVAL, ADAPTATION AND RESISTANCE

The complex social and political meanings surrounding dialect and accent did not escape Jamaican immigrants to the United States. As an American-born girl raised by Jamaican-Americans, my "West Indian accent" was barely detectable to my own ear or to those of most other Americans. However, pronunciation of certain words often would alert strangers from the Caribbean or Africa encountered on the train or bus in New York. They would ask "where you from?" both as a means of creating solidarity and as a way of finding a home in a strange land. Sometimes home meant Africa as well as the Caribbean; foreignness in the United States seemed momentarily to overcome inter-island, ethnic, and national prejudices.

Those first- or second-generation Caribbean Americans who do not have a recognizable Caribbean accent (or who appear not to have one) may find themselves in situations in which they could "pass" as non-Caribbean unless they chose to explicitly acknowledge their background. The dilemmas of this phenomenon are well-known to light-skinned Blacks, who find themselves in situations in which Whites discuss Blacks negatively without being aware that a Black person is present.

Just as accent and dialect can serve different strategic purposes in context, working class Jamaican women immigrants have used various strategies to engage national and international challenges to their survival. As Louise Bennett's humorous poem (quoted at the beginning of Part I) indicates, Jamaicans learned to "colonise in reverse" long ago. As Frantz Fanon has argued, some aspects of these migrations to colonial and neocolonial metropoles are dysfunctional and counterproductive. They evidence a yearning to reject familiar cultural forms in exchange for a wholehearted, but ultimately disappointing, adoption of those of the colonizer.

Nevertheless, some aspects of the migratory urge can also reflect a deliberate desire to retake or redistribute resources at an international level. Jamaican-American women, for example, have attempted to survive and combat sources of oppression that stem, not only from nation-states, but also from global economic and cultural forces.

MIGRATION AND THE AMERICAN DREAM

The pursuit of the American Dream through the attainment of formal citizenship or permanent status can be viewed either as a form of escape or as a form of resistance. The majority of Jamaican women who choose this course must leave their relatives and friends behind, work under difficult and exploitative conditions, navigate the complicated U.S. immigration system, and then learn enough about American history and politics to pass U.S. citizenship exams. Some women hope to escape physically abusive partners; others hope to leave behind the street violence that has plagued Kingston in recent decades. Some were "middle class" teachers or civil servants in Ja maica and were unable to sustain their families on shrinking incomes; they saw years of work in the United States as a domestic or a companion as a necessary evil. Many hope that migration to America will liberate them from economic or social restrictions. While the cultural barriers to work outside the home may not be as strong in Jamaica as in some other countries, social and cultural restrictions on the public behavior of women still exist.

Like other immigrants before them, some Jamaican-American women see assimilation as their best survival strategy. They view conditions in Jamaica as the result of "backwardness" and hope to take advantage of the land of opportunity they believe the United States to be.

Others are not at all naive about the limits of the American Dream for poor Black immigrant women but believe that they have no choice when compared with the conditions they face in Jamaica. Some women learn that migration is not solely a geographic concept: rural women may find themselves in garment assembly plants or private homes in Kingston or New York City more as a result of regional trade agreements than their own preference for one site over another.

Like members of all other voluntary immigrant groups, many make the calculation that their sacrifices will result eventually in a better life for themselves or for their children. Others see this strategy as part of a larger picture. Those who are politically active participate in U.S. elections in the hope that they will be able to change abusive policies. Still others use the relative security of citizenship status as a platform from which to organize among Caribbean and African-American Blacks. Many women participate in local hospital worker unions. Some have fought back against the abuses of the home health care system by forming worker cooperatives and have greater control over their income and working conditions.

REMITTANCES

Most working-class Jamaican women see their legal status in the United States as an opportunity directly or indirectly to address resource inequities in Jamaica itself. In addition to tourism, garment assembly, and the export of sugar and bauxite, the Jamaican economy depends a great deal on the remittances, both cash and in goods that Jamaican women send home to support family and friends. In a country with high inflation and unemployment rates (unemployment reached as high as fifty percent in 1980), the food, clothing, medicine, and money sent home by these women workers are essential.

The United States has played an integral role in connection to the severe economic dislocation caused by structural adjustment policies. One could think of the remittance process as an attempt to retransfer wealth from the North back to the South. At best, this means of transfer has been inefficient. The wealth transfers are not in forms that promote the sustainable development and economic diversification needed in Jamaica and other parts of the Caribbean.

RECREATING HOME

Today, it is not uncommon in East Flatbush to hear accents from Jamaica, Trinidad, Haiti, Korea, Grenada, Puerto Rico, Nigeria, and the Philippines. Flatbush Avenue, a main Brooklyn thoroughfare, is almost impassable on foot or by car seven days a week as shoppers throng the many small businesses on the avenue. Almost every kind of food that could have been purchased at home is available on the street-including stalks of sugar cane. The sounds of reggae and soca music blend with the choral music of the West Indian Pentecostal storefront churches. Yellow taxis are still nowhere to be seen, but licensed and unlicensed Haitian-American cab and van drivers beep their horns hopefully at harried shoppers. Those seeking health care in East Flatbush are certain to encounter nurses' aides, orderlies, and nurses from all parts of the Caribbean.

This frenetic cultural and economic activity takes place in neighborhoods that experience the problems of many other American urban communities, including high crime rates, poor access to public services, and redlining of housing stock. Both petty and more serious crimes have been associated with the advent of crack cocaine and battles among the Jamaican-American "posses" said to control its distribution in those neighborhoods.

Among those women who are cut off from the benefits of the diminishing American social safety net, forms of resistance and survival that originated in Africa and Asia have resurfaced. While much has been made of the lower rates of reliance on public benefits among Caribbean immigrants, those who would use this to divide Black communities fail to examine how it is that these immigrants and their families survive at all.

For example, while many Jamaican-American women are single mothers, many of those who enter the United States to take care of other people's children and parents leave their children in the care of grandmothers or other relatives in Jamaica. The money and goods they send home for the support of their children stretches much further in Jamaica than it could in the United States. Those who have children here often send for other female relatives to share childcare and housekeeping burdens. Those who are undocumented and too poor to gain credit from established banking or other credit institutions join susus, where they pool small amounts of money for consecutive lending. These lending circles, and economic pooling within extended-family networks, can sometimes raise sufficient funds to provide start-up capital for a small business or for the purchase of a home. Unable to find affordable housing through mainstream sources, Jamaican-American women rely on family and church networks to locate rooms or apartments to rent. But even these means of transferring home to a strange land are insufficient to adjust for the fundamental international inequities that necessitate migration, remittances, and immigrant enclave-building.

WHERE ARE THE HUMAN RIGHTS OF JAMAICAN-AMERICAN WOMEN ?

BEYOND BEIJING: FAR FROM HOME

The United Nations Fourth World Conference on Women and the accompanying Non-governmental Forum alternated between two overarching, yet contradictory, narratives about the human rights of women. In one scenario, the Beijing Conference reflected the culmination, or at least the beginning, of a new era of global solidarity. With one voice, women from the far corners of the earth called for the recognition and implementation of gender-specific human rights standards such as those condemning violence against women. In a highly publicized speech to the assembled delegates, Hillary Rodham Clinton announced that the concept of "women's rights as human rights" had finally come into its own. Feminist human rights scholars and activists had begun to blur the distinction between public and private spheres with respect to the application of standards under international human rights law. For example, using this approach, feminists have argued that a government violates the human rights of women if it fails to take measures to deter and punish domestic violence. Correspondingly, feminist human rights activists in the United States also argued successfully that a woman should be granted asylum in the United States if she has a well-founded fear of gender-based violence in her country of origin.

But simultaneously and equally prevalent, a counter narrative of discord arose from differences in culture, race, ethnicity, and economic status among women. This discord took several forms, including the much-debated cultural divide among those taking Universalist approaches to human rights and those taking relativist approaches. Many Third World feminists rejected the characterization by Western feminists of some traditional practices as evidence that Third World cultures are uniquely abusive to the interests of women. They argued that human rights norms should be elaborated and implemented in a cultural context, stressing that pretenses of universalism in the human rights system may mask Western parochialism and imperialism. Other forms of discord have included clashes over the exclusion of feminists of color from national, regional, and global human rights agendas, and conflicts over the relative prioritization of civil and political rights over economic, social, and cultural rights in the West. These conflicts, however, generally are positioned as occurring between two identifiable, geographically defined entities: women from the North versus women from the South.

Yet a third story emerges from Beijing - that of South in North and East in West. This story involves women who cross geographic and cultural borders, carry those borders with them, and recreate their meanings. This less noticed story is that of women with a transnational or international perspective.

Female refugees, displaced persons, migrants, and asylum-seekers often are not full or exclusive members of a single national community. They constantly negotiate borders associated with geography, legal citizenship, racial or ethnic identity, culture, gender roles, or class.

The experiences of Jamaican women immigrants, for example, are shaped by more than the interaction of an easily defined "Jamaican culture" with an equally homogenous "American culture." Rather, they are affected in innumerable ways by African, American, and British cultures (including African-American and Afro-British cultures), tourism, transnational corporations, militarism, the global drug trade, and by other international trade and aid policies before they ever leave the island. "Jamaican" cultural fashions precede them to North America: the dreadlocks and reggae adopted by Jamaican Rastafarian sects can be found in the hair salons and dance clubs of Harlem, Los Angeles, and Toronto as well as in West Kingston. Those who have access to television or radio on the island in turn absorb American cultural images. The identities these Black women hold sometimes relate to political citizenship but more often have to do with power relationships that exceed or make state boundaries invisible. Neither an uncritical universalism nor an insular or exoticized relativism would protect the human rights of women in this context.

HUMAN RIGHTS AND INTERNATIONAL JAMAICAN WOMEN

As subjects of explicit international human rights focus, Jamaican and Jamaican-American women are all but invisible. At the national level, this invisibility stems, in part from Jamaica's status as a "stable parliamentary democracy." In the United States, human rights violations are masked by the irony that while the United States has contributed to the creation of many human rights norms, it has also rejected their internal application.

The U.S. Department of State has identified a number of human rights violations in its reports on human rights practices in Jamaica. Among them are arbitrary arrest and detention, extrajudicial killings, police brutality, and overcrowded prisons. The primary focus of U.S. attention to human rights in Jamaica has been on civil and political rights rather than on the economic, social, and cultural violations with which they co-exist. The existence of widespread domestic violence is noted, but so vaguely described as to be true of most countries in the world: "Violence against women is widespread, but many women are reluctant to acknowledge or report abusive behavior, leading to wide variations in estimates of its extent." Ironically, police officials have attempted to calm the fears of potential tourists, by blaming the high murder rates in Jamaica on domestic violence.

The primary nongovernmental human rights organization in the country, the Jamaica Council on Human Rights, is under constant threat of closure due to lack of resources and political harassment. At the same time, both private and government interest in the United States and Jamaica find it essential to maintain the island's image as a tourist playground. A 1992 human rights report on Jamaica by the Lawyers Committee for Human Rights noted the following:

> Although tourists in the resort areas are generally insulated from violent crime, the extraordinary incidence of extrajudicial killings and police abuse appears to be directly linked to efforts to protect the $740 million per year tourist industry.... Further, the State Department report does not address the underlying socioeconomic conditions associated with an increase in crime. High unemployment rates, overcrowding in urban areas due to migration from agricultural areas, devalued currency, and skyrocketing prices for even basic food items, all contribute to crime.

The failure to focus on economic and social violations and the desire to maintain a tourist-friendly image has masked violations of women's rights in Jamaica. The declining availability of land for subsistence farming has forced many rural women to migrate to already overcrowd urban centers in search of work. Those who work in export processing trade zone apparel assembly plants are subject to low wages, dangerous working conditions, and reprisals for attempting to organize among themselves. "Higglers," who once primarily traded in crops from small subsistence farms they or their husbands now trade in small imported items for retail sale on the street. They can be forced off the street if they set up too close to a formal business or made to pay licensing fees or payoffs to local police. Domestic violence continues to be viewed as a private matter which is often ignored by the police, given the already overcrowded prisons and the greater publicity surrounding gang-related crimes.

The majority of Jamaican women who immigrate to the United States do so for economic reasons. Therefore, they generally do not appeal to U.S. legal protections for refuge and asylum. While they may find economic conditions somewhat better than at home, life for them is by no means easy. Those who are "unskilled" must find work with an employer willing to sponsor them. They must then endure the wait for permanent residency status. Some may experience sexual violence or other abuses in the homes of their employers, but many fear that reporting such violations risks deportation or lengthened waiting periods for legalization. For similar reasons, undocumented women who believe that marriage to an American citizen will protect them from deportation sometimes find themselves afraid to leave an abusive husband. Often of questionable immigration status, some working-class Jamaican-American women are denied access to everything from health care to bank loans. While some of these women may be favored over native-born Blacks by employers who know them to be Caribbean American, they are not immune from race, gender, and class discrimination.

Given the range of harms facing Jamaican and Jamaican-American women, one may well ask whether a feminist human rights framework such as that of the Women's Convention, is helpful to them. Jamaica, along with 154 other countries, has ratified the Women's Convention and protects against sex discrimination in its constitution. Although U.S. ratification has been long in coming, there is support for it under the current administration. While CEDAW is considered one of the most progressive international human rights instruments, and its ratification in the United States likely would be hailed as a positive step, it still would embody significant limitations in addressing the conditions under which many working-class Jamaican-American women exist.

CEDAW, which uses an antidiscrimination framework to address the subordination of women, is indeed revolutionary in its approach. It requires recognition of economic and social, as well as civil and political, rights. It further calls on state parties to take "appropriate" measures to eliminate sex discrimination in both public and private settings. It also provides for a specific focus on the needs of rural women. Finally, it recognizes the roles of women in both political and family life. The Committee charged with its implementation has been noted for the seriousness with which it takes the analysis of reports by state parties and for the feminist sensibilities of its members.

Nevertheless, CEDAW also has well-known structural limitations. The most important of these, the lack of an optional protocol for individual complaints, is under review by a special working group at the time of this writing. However, enhancing the relevance of CEDAW for Jamaican women immigrants in the United States would require more than the addition of an individual complaint procedure or other traditional structural reforms.

Although CEDAW does address the behavior of private actors, it does so by obligating state parties to implement human rights protections. In the case of Jamaican women, however, responsibility for rights violations may be difficult to place. Who should be accountable, for example, when a woman is driven to work in the informal sector for her subsistence? She may have been forced to leave land on which she had engaged in subsistence farming in favor of its use for cash crop or tourist activities. One could argue that a government that allowed or encourages transnational corporations to purchase her land for less than fair compensation might have violated CEDAW. Under feminist approaches to human rights, the state also would be considered responsible if it allowed that woman to be brutalized by police as they clear the streets for traditional retailers.

However, Jamaica, like other Caribbean nations, is not an autonomous actor, particularly with respect to economic policy. The responsibility under human rights laws of entities like the World Trade Organization, the World Bank, and the International Monetary Fund and that of transnational corporations themselves, has not yet been fully developed.

Similarly, in the United States, even the long hoped-for ratification of CEDAW would leave many questions unanswered with respect to the human rights of inter/national Black women. Which nation-state-the host country or the sending country-bears responsibility when women are forced to migrate to survive? Of which chapter is it a violation to be forced to leave children behind in search of a living wage? Does "domestic violence as a human rights violation" include violence against the "domestic" ? Can an instrument intended to protect against discrimination against women on the basis of sex adequately address discrimination on the basis of both race and gender? Because the violations they experience do not bear an easy relationship to traditional controls on state power, Jamaican women immigrants have had to find innovative ways of resisting the violation of their rights and redeploying power.

CEDAW, and similar liberal feminist approaches to human rights, do not lack value for the women in question. Arguably, the contributions of feminist approaches, whether liberal or progressive, have led to some of the most exciting and innovative changes in the international human rights system. Instruments such as CEDAW have explicitly required state parties to adopt effective measures, both legislative and otherwise, to combat public and private discrimination against women. After Vienna and Beijing, it now seems commonplace for official UN meetings to be accompanied by large gatherings of nongovernmental organizations. Perhaps most importantly, these efforts have led to the kind of consciousness raising that encourages worldwide debate on which policies and actions constitute violations of women's human rights and what should be done to end them.

Undermining these promising developments, however, is the reality that, in post-Cold War context, even the familiar roles of states as sources either of oppression or of protection have been replaced by new actors and influences. Regional trade entities and transnational corporations have a great deal to do with the human rights of women and men. Yet these organizations often claim that they are nonpolitical and deem themselves outside the international human rights framework. Thus, U.S. and Jamaican government, for international human rights, is largely contingent on their transnational economic priorities.

JAMAICAN-AMERICAN WOMEN AND CRITICAL RACE FEMINISM

Critical race theorists have critiqued the tendency to view non-Black peoples of color through the lenses of essentialized immigration status or "foreignness." Their work wrestles with the implications of U.S. immigration policy and the renewal of old debates about the roles and status of immigrants in American society. However, even critical race scholarship that focuses on immigration status so far has paid little attention to the implications of the presence in the United States of Blacks from other parts of the African Diaspora. The complex realities facing Jamaican-American women, therefore, remain largely unexamined.

As a branch of critical race scholarship, critical race feminist scholarship identifies the dangers of essentialism in American anti-racist and anti-sexist law and politics. It analyzes how race-based and gender-based discrimination can combine to form more than the sum of their parts. In addition, many have demonstrated how discrimination against immigrants, sexual minorities, and people with disabilities, also intersect to intensify race- and gender-based oppression. Further, critical race feminist scholarship has elaborated ways in which the urge to essentialize makes the particular experiences of women of color invisible within broader communities.

The insights of critical race feminist studies with regard to the multiple impacts of race, gender, class, and language could have particular resonance for Black women immigrants given that they encounter multiple identity discrimination.

For example, critical race feminist scholarship challenges the notion that U.S. citizenship immunizes Black women from the violation of their human rights. It also challenges negative images and stereotypes of Black women. Both approaches have relevance for the analysis of the status of Black Jamaican-American women.

U.S. CITIZENSHIP AND JAMAICAN-AMERICAN WOMEN

The participation of Jamaican-American women in the prospective benefits of residence in the United States is limited by the labels attached to their immigration status-"undocumented aliens," visa "overstays," "permanent residents," or "naturalized" citizens. Women immigrants must make their way through a complex and abusive maze of federal and state regulations that target immigrants, whether "legal" or "illegal."

Whatever form of legal citizenship status Jamaican women immigrants "choose," as Black women, their full participation in American society is limited by discrimination and by the narrowing scope of legal responses to white supremacist and patriarchal agendas. Since the nation's founding, those in power have worked to exclude one group or another from full citizenship in the United States. Native Americans, African Americans, Asian Americans, ethnic and religious minorities from Europe, Puerto Ricans, and Haitian Americans-all have been denied the privileges of full citizenship at one time or another.

For African Americans, this exclusion from the benefits of citizenship originated in the history of Black enslavement in the United States. The denial of the citizenship rights of chattel slaves was enshrined by constitutional provision and by judicial interpretation. The impact of that history, along with the related histories of global imperialism and neo-colonialism, continues to plague modern-day Blacks whether they are descended from slaves in the United States, Latin America, or the Caribbean, or whether their ancestors were never enslaved at all.

Jamaican-American women share a legacy of slavery. Still, many people who enter the United States from predominantly Black countries, experience the unique aspects of American race and gender politics in ways that are new to them. Critical race feminism has contributed to the analysis of the legal enshrinement of sub-human, non-citizen status to Blacks in the United States by analyzing the particular historical and modern implications for Black women. Critical race feminist scholarship could profitably expand its exploration of the implications of the problematic nature of U.S. citizenship status for native-born Black women to Black immigrant women. To challenge the second-class nature of U.S. citizenship for Black women, however, native-born and immigrant Black women must overcome divisions within our own communities.

CROSSING BARRIERS: ADDRESSING STEREOTYPES

Much has been made in the writings of conservative sociologists and political economists, of the relative economic success, as measured by employment levels, home ownership rates, and non-reliance on public assistance, of Caribbean-American Blacks as compared to native-born Blacks. Those social scientists argue that this difference is due primarily to a unique "Caribbean culture." They use this conclusion to suggest that race discrimination in the United States would be overcome if native-born Blacks would merely adopt such cultural practices. Other economists and sociologists have suggested that those statistical differences, if accurate, are due to a variety of factors including: (1) class and educational differences among those able to migrate in different time periods; (2) the high motivation of those individuals who are willing to migrate, whether they move from the Caribbean to the United States or from one part of the United States to another; (3) the racist search by some employers for a "better Black" who is perceived to be a more docile or reliable worker; and (4) the use of new immigrant groups as a middle tier between native-born Blacks and Whites. To the extent that economic success can be attributed to both male and female immigrants, Kasinitz points out that the majority of Blacks are still worse off than the majority of native-born Whites.

Nevertheless, the actual or perceived differences among native-born and immigrant Black communities create special challenges for critical race feminist analysis. The goal of promoting social justice among those at the intersections of identity-based oppressions is made more difficult as those identities appear to be more complex. American politicians and business managers have found it convenient to essentialize Blacks as a monolithic group or to overemphasize dissimilarities between West Indians and Black Americans when it suits their purposes. Even more troubling, however, is that both native-born and Caribbean-born Blacks internalize these constructions in ways that undermine projects of social change, including efforts to apply international human rights strategies to the United States.

Some Caribbean Americans may not only incorporate positive stereotypes in their self-image, but also interweave them with prevailing negative stereotypes of native-born Blacks, including Black women. In both domestic and international popular media, native-born American Black women are portrayed as lazy, overly reliant on welfare, baby factories, and criminals.

Critical race feminist scholarship has exposed and attacked the racism and sexism underpinnings of such stereotypes. However, work remains to be done in deconstructing the artificial images that divide native-born and foreign-born Black communities. Ironically, stereotypes that have similar origins are applied to Black women in international contexts. For example, Black women in the Caribbean, like many in the Third World, are also stereotyped by Westerners as having too many children. Coercive population policies and experimental birth control methods often make their way to poor minority communities in the United States after being tried on Third World women first. Those women who desire to escape poverty at home by migrating are viewed as potential drains on the American economy.

By contrast, once they arrive in the United States, casting Jamaican-American women immigrants as hard workers is central to their image as members of a "model minority." But they soon find that model-minority status is a double-edged sword. To some employers, the "better Black" is merely a young woman who will work for low wages because she fears deportation. The notion that Jamaican-American women are strong, yet nurturing, also may mean that they are considered impervious to harm and therefore more likely to perform unattractive work for inadequate compensation. The accents of some Jamaican- American women may give them a "leg-up" in certain employment contexts. In others, an identifiably non-American accent may expose them to hostility in an environment that rejects multiculturalism and multilingualism in the United States.

The failure to challenge and deconstruct stereotypes can lead to almost comical contradictions in popular imagery of Jamaican-American women. In the popular imagination, they are simultaneously hardworking, industrious homeowners and "mules" for ultraviolet "drug posses." They are said to be conservative in their religious beliefs, yet ready to respond to sexual harassment with ribald back talk. They are nurturing and supportive caregivers as nurses and nannies, but they are also bad mothers who have too many children. They are simultaneously over-educated elites and a ready labor reserve for low-wage work.

Such contradictory stereotyping is familiar to many native-born Blacks as well. When convenient, Black women in the

United States have been stereotyped as strong-willed and independent or as abusive to the self-esteem of Black men. They are targeted as lazy and yet are relied on to serve as a vast resource for low-wage labor. Their images adorn the covers of magazines discussing welfare reform, even though the majority of recipients of welfare are White. Even the involvement of a Black female law professor in a national political controversy had to be filtered through competing stereotypes of Black women. An important task facing critical race feminist scholarship, therefore, is to reveal how the images of native-born and immigrant women of color are manipulated and how the women themselves are moved around like chess pieces to suit hidden political agendas.

The apparent security provided by U.S. citizenship status and immigrant community cohesiveness ultimately will be of limited value to Jamaican-American women. As Black women, their citizenship is stunted by the intersection of racism and sexism in this society. As workers, they are subject to the limited ability of formal labor standards to ensure that they are paid a living wage, work under safe conditions, and have adequate benefits. Further, as immigrants or the descendants of immigrants, their ability to work in solidarity with the U.S. Black community also may be threatened by hostility from other Blacks or by their own desire to separate.

Critical race feminist scholarship has previously demonstrated how Black women are discriminated against in ways that layer and enhance both racial and gender discrimination. I have argued that this approach can also address the racial politics of their U.S. immigration status. Nevertheless, even adding the axis of immigration status to the analysis is not sufficient.

Depending on the context, Black women immigrants from Haiti may be treated differently (or the same) as those from Jamaica. Black women immigrants from Brazil may be treated differently (or the same) as those from Cuba. All of them may be treated differently (or the same) as those from Nigeria or Cape Verde. The particularities of their experiences, however, must be recognized in order to build coalitions on solid ground. Equally as important, however, critical race feminism also must address the inter/national connections among the violations of the human rights of Black women.

The final challenge facing critical race feminist scholars, therefore, is to reinterrogate both the essentialization and the false dichotomization of Black women. One useful means of doing so is to test the limits of the international human rights framework by taking it places where it has, so far, been reluctant to go-simultaneously toward identifying violations of human rights within the United States and beyond state-centered geographic and political boundaries.

CONCLUSION

This chapter has analyzed how the status of working-class Jamaican- American women can slip through the cracks of two analytical frameworks. It has argued that both frameworks could be applied in ways that would be of greater benefit to one group of Black immigrants. Feminist human rights approaches must take greater account of the influence of race and ethnicity on the human rights of women. Critical race feminism must address the role of Black immigrant women in American society. Greater attention to the violations of political and economic rights in the United States is one way of doing so.

Most significantly, however, both the human rights framework and the critical race feminist framework must shed light on the non-state and interstate actors that influence the conditions under which the majority of women of color live.

The hypocritical failure to fully address violations of the rights of subordinated groups within the United States has been criticized at least since the Cold War. Similarly, concerns about the role of Western imperialism in the application of international human rights standards to the Third World have been expressed even prior to the drafting of the Universal Declaration of Human Rights. However, violations of the human rights of subordinated groups even within the

United States are perpetrated by forces that do not emanate from fixed geographic locations. To be effective, responses to those abuses of power, therefore, must occur in constantly shifting forms.

Critical race scholars recently have begun to make efforts to internationalize the impact of the critical race movement. In doing so, they have begun to work with human rights and post-colonial theorists on ways to cultivate a deeper understanding of domestic identity politics. Still, those efforts primarily analyze issues of identity and social justice from the perspective of traditional geopolitical divides. They raise questions about the relevance of the experiences and political strategies of subordinated groups in the North (the United States) for those in the South (South Africa). They also investigate, in comparative perspective, the relevance of post-colonial contradictions for marginalized groups in the United States. Both pursuits involve important and useful agendas for legal scholarship.

This chapter calls for the addition of another, complementary, approach. It recognizes the continued importance of identity categories despite the complexity of their construction, but it also calls for increased attention to the changing nature of the forces that subordinate those identity groups.

Recent attacks on the human rights of the poor, women, immigrants, and people of color in the United States, for example, have taken on an international flavor. "Welfare reform" legislation, which targeted poor women of color, included provisions to deny poor immigrants, including the elderly and disabled, access to public benefits. Anti-terrorism legislation seemed to stem from the same nativist roots as anti-immigrant legislation. The specter of the deportation of real or imagined "criminals" from the U.S. to Jamaica raised questions about local crime control policies in Jamaica as well as about reductions in remittances. U.S. and European trade policy toward the Caribbean intersected with questions about U.S. campaign finance reform.

The implications of these interconnections remain to be explored for international women. The human rights of both native born and immigrant women of color are violated when the denial of public entitlements is justified by reference to the stereotype of the "undeserving welfare mother." When Third World governments make cuts in public sector supports in response to structural adjustment policies, how are the rights of workers in the United States affected? Does the positioning of Jamaican-American women as superhuman rebel women, make them less in need of the human rights protections against gender violence? How should Jamaican-American women engage questions of economic and social rights as members of a model minority in the United States when their families and friends in Jamaica suffer under the effects of structural adjustment policies? How should the "success" of some Jamaican women immigrants be analyzed when that success comes at the cost of long hours of backbreaking work for low wages and at the cost of separation from their families? These questions illustrate the cross-boundary nature of the problem: not merely how to account for the presence of Black immigrant women in feminist human rights and critical race approaches, but also how to extend the analysis to address international sources of human rights violations.

Legal scholarship by and about Black women and other women of color only recently has come into its own; there are still rich veins of knowledge about women of color that remain to be mined. One of those areas of inquiry is the effects of globalization on women of color in international contexts. Globalization in its current forms makes the old constructs of "domestic" and "foreign" less relevant than the task of identifying common patterns of oppression. This task requires that subordinated groups look up long enough from fighting over the scraps from the table to see the abundance of food being wasted just above our heads. It means seeing ourselves in the other and the other in ourselves. Finally, we must recognize both how "we" (Black women) are not as cohesive and monolithic as we thought and how "they" (Black immigrant women) are not so easily distinguished from "us."

I began this discussion from the perspective of Jamaican women immigrants because it has special resonance for me. However, it might have been equally useful to start the discussion from the perspectives of Blacks, women, the international, the poor, Jamaicans, immigrants, victims of human rights violations, or a number of other identities common to this artificially constructed group.

It is crucial, therefore, to overcome barriers to the formation of strategic progressive coalitions among subordinated groups. Such efforts to build and recreate coalitions around common concerns are among the most important forms of resistance to oppression available to us. At a time when the poor, women, and people of color are under attack on all fronts, it is more important than ever to bridge old gaps and fissures in the path to social change.

6

Women's Rights
A Global Issue

Women's rights around the world are an important indicator of understanding global well-being. Many may think that women's rights are only an issue in countries where religion is law, such as many Muslim countries. Or even worse, some may think this is no longer an issue at all. But reading this report about the United Nation's Women's Treaty and how an increasing number of countries are lodging reservations will show otherwise.

A report from *Human Rights Watch* also describes how women's rights have not been observed in some countries as much as expected; in some places claims are made that women's rights will be respected more, yet policies are sometimes not changed enough or at all - thus still undermining the rights of women.

In some patriarchal societies, religion or tradition can be used as a barrier for equal rights. For example, as *Inter Press Service* reported, the Bangladesh government tried to hide behind laws to deny women equal rights. In Pakistan for example, honor killings directed at women have been carried for even the slightest reasons.

As *Amnesty International* also points out, "Governments are not living up to their promises under the Women's Convention to protect women from discrimination and violence such as rape and female genital mutilation." There are many governments who have also not ratified the

Convention, including the U.S. Many countries that have ratified it do so with many reservations.

Despite the almost universal ratification of the Convention (second only to the Convention on the Rights of the Child), a number of countries have still not signed or ratified it. The handful of remaining countries are: USA (signed, but not ratified), Iran, Qatar, Cook Islands (a Non-member state of the United Nations), Nauru, Palau, Tonga, Somalia, and Sudan.

To see the US on this list may seem surprising to most, and *Human Rights Watch* is critical of the delay in getting ratification, noting that this treaty has been in limbo in the U.S. Senate for *decades.* It was sent to the Senate Foreign Relations Committee for a vote in 1980.

The first hearing on it was 10 years later. After a vote mostly in favor for it by the Foreign Relations Committee in 1994, some conservative senators blocked a US Senate vote on it. In 2002 the Foreign Relations Committee again voted that the treaty should be ratified, but the 107th Congress ended, so it requires a vote again in favor of sending the treaty to the full Senate for ratification.

Some opponents of the treaty have raised fears that it would undermine US law, but *Amnesty International USA* shows that such fears of the treaty are based on myths.

The US of course has a decent record when it comes to women's rights, so this may not seem a concern immediately. However, as *Amnesty International USA* further argues not only would ratification for the US be straight forward (for US laws in this area are already consistent with the CEDAW treaty), but it would also help to increase their credibility when raising these issues worldwide.

WOMEN WORK MORE THAN MEN BUT PAID LESS

According to *Inter Press Service*, "On a global scale, women cultivate more than half of all the food that is grown. In sub-Saharan Africa and the Caribbean, they produce up to 80 percent of basic foodstuffs. In Asia, they account for around 50 percent of food production. In Latin America, they are mainly engaged in subsistence farming, horticulture, poultry and raising small livestock."

Yet women often get little recognition for that. In fact, many go unpaid. It is very difficult for these women to get the financial resources required to buy equipment etc, as many societies still do not accept, or realize, that there is a change in the "traditional" roles. UNICEF's 2007 report on state of the world's children focused on the discrimination and disempowerment women face throughout their lives and how that impacts children's lives.

Reasons for such disparity include the fact that women are generally underpaid and because they often perform low-status jobs, compared to men. UNICEF notes that the data isn't always perfect, and that generalizations such as the above can hide wider fluctuations. "In Brazil, for example, women under the age of 25 earn a higher average hourly wage than their male counterparts."

UNICEF's main summary of equality in employment included the following points: For many women, unpaid work in and for the household takes up the majority of their working hours, with much less time spent in remunerative employment. Even when they participate in the labour market for paid employment, women still undertake the majority of the housework.

When women work outside the household, they earn, on average, far less than men. They are also more likely to work in more precarious forms of employment with low earnings, little financial security and few or no social benefits.

Women not only earn less than men but also tend to own fewer assets. Smaller salaries and less control over household income constrain their ability to accumulate capital. Gender biases in property and inheritance laws and in other channels of acquiring assets also leave women and children at greater risk of poverty.

Paid employment for women does not automatically lead to better outcomes for children. Factors such as the amount of time women spend working outside the household, the conditions under which they are employed and who controls the income they generate determine how the work undertaken by women in the labour market affects their own well-being and that of children.

GENDER DISCRIMINATION THROUGHOUT A LIFETIME

The above-mentioned 2007 report on state of the world's had an informative section on how women are discriminated against at various stages through life, summarized here:

Foeticide and infanticide

UNICEF notes that "Where there is a clear economic or cultural preference for sons, the misuse of pregnancy diagnostic tools can facilitate female foeticide."

The middle years

"A principal focus of the middle years of childhood and adolescence is ensuring access to, and completion of, quality primary and secondary education. With a few exceptions, it is mostly girls who suffer from educational disadvantage."

Adolescence

"Among the greatest threats to adolescent development are abuse, exploitation and violence, and the lack of vital knowledge about sexual and reproductive health, including HIV/AIDS." Specific areas that UNICEF highlighted were female genital mutilation/cutting; child marriage and premature parenthood; sexual abuse, exploitation and trafficking; sexual and reproductive health; and HIV/AIDS.

Motherhood and old age

These are "two key periods in many women's lives when the pernicious effects of both poverty and inequality can combine." Shockingly, "It is estimated that each year more than half a million women-roughly one woman every minute-die as a result of pregnancy complications and childbirth," 99% of which occur in developing countries. Yet "many of these women's lives could be saved if they had access to basic health care services." In addition, elderly women may face double discrimination on the basis of both gender and age. Many older women are plunged into poverty at a time of life when they are very vulnerable. However, "children's rights are advanced when programmes that seek to benefit children and families also include elderly women."

FEMINIZATION OF POVERTY

The "feminization of poverty" is a phenomenon that is unfortunately on the increase. Basically, women are increasingly the ones who suffer the most poverty.

Professor of anthropology, Richard Robbins also notes that, at the same time that women produce 75 to 90 percent of food crops in the world, they are responsible for the running of households. According to the United Nations, in no country in the world do men come anywhere close to women in the amount of time spent in housework. Furthermore, despite the efforts of feminist movements, women in the core [wealthiest, Western countries] still suffer disproportionately, leading to what sociologist refers to as the "feminization of poverty," where two out of every three poor adults are women. The informal slogan of the Decade of Women became "Women do two-thirds of the world's work, receive 10 percent of the world's income and own 1 percent of the means of production."

This then also affects children, which makes the dire situation even worse. For example, even in the richest country in the world, the USA, the poorest are women caring for children.

The lending strategies to developing countries by

institutions such as the IMF and World Bank have affected many women in those countries.

Poverty, trade and economic issues are very much related to women's rights issues due to the impacts they can have. Tackling these issues as well also helps to tackle women's rights issues. And, tackling gender issues helps tackle poverty-related issues.

WOMEN AND CHILDREN: THE DOUBLE DIVIDEND OF GENDER EQUALITY

The above title comes from UNICEF's 2007 report on state of the world's children where they focus on the discrimination and disempowerment women face throughout their lives and how those impacts children's lives. The key messages that came out from the report were as follows:

i. Gender equality and the well-being of children go hand in hand.

ii. Gender equality furthers the cause of child survival and development.

iii. Gender equality produces a double dividend: It benefits both women and children.

iv. Healthy, educated and empowered women have healthy, educated and confident daughters and sons. Gender equality will not only empower women to overcome poverty and live full and productive lives, but will better the lives of children, families and countries as well.

v. Women's equal rights and influence in the key decisions that shape their lives and those of children must be enhanced in three distinct arenas: the household, the workplace and the political sphere.

vi. A change for the better in any one of these realms influences women's equality in the others, and has a profound and positive impact on child's well-being and development.

vii. Gender equality is not only morally right, it is pivotal to human progress and sustainable development.

viii. Achieving Millennium Development Goal Number 3 - promoting gender equality and empowering women- will also contribute to achieving all the other goals, from reducing poverty and hunger to saving children's lives, improving maternal health, ensuring universal education, combating HIV/AIDS, malaria and other diseases, and ensuring environmental sustainability.

WOMEN AND THE MEDIA

Even media attention on women who help and fight for certain causes is distorted. For example, Fairness and Accuracy. In Reporting (FAIR) analyzed U.S. media reporting during the British Princess Diana's funeral, and noted that the U.S. media typically concentrate only on a few people like the late Diana and Mother Teresa who had some sort of celebrity type status, and rarely reported on the thousands of others doing similar work.

In other cases, the roles of women presented in the media, from talk shows, to entertainment shows as well as news reporting can often end up reinforcing the status quo and the cultural stereotypes, which influence other women to follow suit. This happens in all nations, from the wealthiest to the poorest (and happens with men as well as children). It can have positive aspects, such as providing guidance and sharing issues etc. but it can also have a negative effect of continuing inherent prejudices etc.

BEIJING +5 SPECIAL SESSION

From June 5 to June 9 2000, there was a conference at the United Nations, New York, continuing on 5 years from a similar conference in Beijing, 1995. (The formal name of the conference was "Women: 2000: Gender Equality, Development and Peace for the Twenty-First Century.")

In 1985 there was a conference in Nairobi, Kenya, to formulate strategies for advancing women's rights. This was followed by a "plan of action" defined in 1995, in Beijing.

It has been recognized and agreed for a while that successful development also involves gender equality. The goals of this conference then were to reflect on the promised provisions of equality, development and peace for all women everywhere.

Leading up to, and during the conference, many organizations had numerous issues to bring to the fore, including:

i. Women's reproductive rights
ii. Abduction of girls
iii. Child soldiers and armed conflict
iv. Poverty and Economy
v. Education and Training
vi. Health
vii. Violence
viii. Decision Making
ix. Institutional Mechanisms
x. Human Rights
xi. Media
xii. Environment
xiii. The Girl-child

According to a UN report, the international community had fallen far short of its commitments to empower women and achieve gender equality and that only eight out of 188 member states had certain global agreements for this.

It was also pointed out at this UN session that Women continued to be deprived of basic and fundamental rights because of measures imposed in certain countries.

In fact, some were even opposed to moving forward on such important issues, such as Holy See (the Vatican), Nicaragua, Sudan and Libya and sometimes Iraq and various other nations on particular issues such as reproductive rights, even freedom of expression (Libya and the Vatican opposed this). The Vatican, Iran and some other delegations even wanted to delete references to sexual and reproductive rights and health in the Current Challenges section of the review document.

Regarding the Vatican (the Holy See), there was growing concern at their role as permanent observer, where they are considered to be more than a non-governmental organization (NGO), but less than a nation. They therefore have some influence and have been criticized at the way they have affected some UN decisions regarding gender-related issues to be more effectively pushed forward. As part of some of the criticisms, there is the suggestion to challenge the Holy sees power by demanding that the Vatican should be classified as an NGO instead.

Some NGOs and organizations from the third world trying to fight for women's rights also felt they were left out of the conference.

WOMEN, MILITARISM AND VIOLENCE

It is often argued-and accepted-that women, being the "gentler sex", and typically being the main care givers in society, are less aggressive than men. Feminists often argue that women, if given appropriate and full rights, could counter-balance a male-dominated world which is characterized by aggression in attitudes, thoughts, society and, ultimately, war.

In May 2004, the Occupation/Coalition forces in Iraq were shown around the world to be committing torture and other grotesque acts on Iraqi captives. For feminists and others, what was also shocking was that some of these acts were being perpetrated by women in the U.S. military.

Feminist activist Barbara Ehrenreich captures some of the thoughts and reactions quite well:

Secretly, I hoped that the presence of women in the U.S. army would over time change the military, making it more respectful of other people and cultures, more capable of genuine peacekeeping. That's what I thought, but I don't think that anymore.

Certain kind of feminism, or perhaps should say a certain kind of feminist naivete, died in Abu Ghraib [the prison facility from where most of the torture pictures and footage originated]. It was a feminism that saw men as the perpetual perpetrators, women as the perpetual victims and male sexual violence against women as the root of all injustice. Rape has repeatedly been an instrument of war and, to some feminists; it was beginning to look as if war was an extension of rape. There seemed to be at least some evidence that male sexual sadism was connected to our species' tragic propensity for violence. That was before we had seen female sexual sadism in action.

... But the assumption [within feminism] of [women's] superiority [over men], or at least a lesser inclination toward cruelty and violence, was more or less beyond debate. After all, women do most of the caring work in our culture, and in polls are consistently less inclined toward war than men.

... If that assumption had been accurate, then all we would have had to do to make the world a better place-kinder, less violent, more just-would have been to assimilate into what had been, for so many centuries, the world of men.

... What we need is a tough new kind of feminism with no illusions. Women do not change institutions simply by assimilating into them, only by consciously deciding to fight for change. We need a feminism that teaches a woman to say no-not just to the date rapist or overly insistent boyfriend but, when necessary, to the military or corporate hierarchy within which she finds herself.

Towards the end of the article, Ehrenreich notes that gender equality often appears to be limited to allowing women to have equality in a male-dominated world, meaning women struggle to have rights to do what men do. But, if what men are doing is generally seen as negative, then gender equality in that context is not enough. As she ends:

> To cite an old, and far from naive, feminist saying: "If you think equality is the goal, your standards are too low." It is not enough to be equal to men, when the men are acting like beasts. It is not enough to assimilate. We need to create a world worth assimilating into.

7

Global Human Rights Defense

Global Human Rights Defence (GHRD) is an international human rights Non-Governmental Organisation (NGO) working with and for minorities.

GHRD specifically addresses those areas and populations of the world where severe and extensive human rights violations of certain ethnic, linguistic and religious minorities have taken place for long periods, and where structural help and global attention of the international media have proven to be absent or insufficient. GHRD conducts its work via three pillars:

i. Human rights reporting: done by local observers.

ii. Humanitarian aid: aimed at victims of human rights.

iii. Human rights education: in South-Asia, Netherlands and Europe.

MINORITIES

GHRD concentrates on the human rights of minority groups:

i. That are dominated by social, economical and political power;

ii. That have been deprived of effective protection against gross and systematic violations; and

iii. That have been deprived of access to resources simply because of their identity and beliefs.

GHRD's work is based on the UN Declaration on Rights of Minorities (1992), and therefore it works with linguistic, religious and ethnic minorities. "Basic aims of the United Nations, as proclaimed in the Charter, is to promote and encourage respect for human rights and for fundamental freedoms for all, without distinction as to race, sex, language or religion, emphasizing that the constant promotion and realization of the rights of persons belonging to national or ethnic, religious and linguistic minorities, as an integral part of the development of society as a whole and within a democratic framework based on the rule of law, would contribute to the strengthening of friendship and cooperation among peoples and States" General Assembly Resolution 47/135, 18 December 1992.

IDENTITY

GHRD is integrally distinctive from other organisations in various ways. For one, it focuses on those issues and areas where people have been deprived of their rights without their cases being properly addressed by both governments and authorities. GHRD is the first organisation in The Hague (The Netherlands) to address specifically the human rights of minorities. Outside The Hague, GHRD is distinctive because of its permanent presence of local observers, who produce genuine information and reports of distinctive quality, due to their profound knowledge of the local humanitarian situation.

MISSION

It is the mission of GHRD to actively promote human rights, especially minority rights (in accordance with the UN Declaration on Rights of Minorities), as well as to form a well-structured international platform to inform, influence and demand efforts from established organisations and relevant authorities.

OBJECTIVES

GHRD has formulated the following objectives in order to fulfill its mission:

i. To fight against the violation of human rights of minority groups, particularly in those areas and populations where structural help or global attention of the world has not been given;

ii. To provide refugee centre assistance and humanitarian aid to those who lack elementary basic needs such as food, clothing, shelter and proper sanitary conditions; and

iii. To develop, stimulate and enhance human rights awareness in a national and international perspective, through means of education.

HISTORY

GHRD was officially founded after The Hague 2003 International Conference on Human Rights, which were sub-themed Human Rights of Refugees and Victims of Ethnic and Religious Violence. At the end of the conference a gap in the human rights work was spotted: human rights of minorities. The establishment of GHRD was supported by a broad spectrum of over a 150 selected participants of national and international human rights organisations from all over the world. The memorandum of association, which was agreed upon unanimously and signed by all participating parties, provides the structure of this international organisation.

At the time of its establishment, the Boar was lead by Sradhanand Sital who still is the chairman of the organisation. Rohit Oemrawsingh was the Secretary and Suzanne Girbarak the Treasurer. Ranjeev Gowri has volunteered during the congress and was taken on board of the new project as well.

When it was first established, GHRD had no official office and worked solely on a voluntary basis. Meetings were held at the founders' living-rooms and activities were conducted by a small group of dedicated people.

A few months after the founding of GHRD, Nizaad Bissumbhar comes across the organisation at an event and immediately joins the cause. Bissumbhar and Gowri soon become active members of GHRD.

In September 2005, the organisation opened its head-office in The Hague at Javastraat and employed the first paid staff. In the building, GHRD was neighbour of United Network of Young Peace builders (UNOY) and United Nations High Commission for Refugees (UNHCR).

Also in 2005, GHRD promoted a four-day congress at the City Hall of the Hague. The congress was titled GHRD reaches for the future and brought together some 120 experts in the field of human rights. Amongst the speakers were Dutch Human Rights Ambassador Mr. P. de Klerk, and the Mayor of The Hague Mr. W. Deetman.

In 2006, Oemrawsingh and Girbarak leave the Board and Bissumbhar and Gowri take their respective positions as Secretary and Treasurer of the Board.

The founders had already some contacts in South-Asia and it was easier to start acting in the region. Moreover, the South-Asia region fulfilled the mission/vision of GHRD, as the violations of human rights of minorities did not hit the headlines nor were they on top of the political agenda.

OFFICES

GHRD head-office is based in The Hague, The Netherlands, where all operations from the region are coordinated. At the time of its establishment, GHRD initially opened its offices in India, and Bangladesh. Nepal and Sri Lanka followed in 2004. Except Sri Lanka, all the offices are still active. The Sri Lanka's office had to be closed after the Tsunami on December 2004. After the disaster, a great number of NGOs started working in the country and employing local human rights experts. As a small organisation, GHRD was not able to top the salaries being paid to the locals and had to abandon the country.

In 2006, GHRD opened officially the Bhutan Chapter. GHRD had been working with the Bhutanese refugees in Nepal from the start. The observer based in Kathmandu worked closely with the seven refugee camps sponsored by the United Nations High Commission for Refugees (UNHCR).

In the same year, in India the Women's Wing was launched. However, due to a lack of human resources, the division was never fully activated. GHRD has also contacts spread around Malaysia and Indonesia and is currently studying the possibility of opening an office in Pakistan. In July 2007, GHRD signed a letter of intent for exchange of information with the African foundation Bajito Onda Africa.

STOP THE GANG RAPES CAMPAIGN

In 2007 GHRD started its first campaign. The initiative focused on the gang rapes that victimized Bangladeshi women and young girls. The main objective of the campaign was to raise awareness to the issue. The campaign was based in the Netherlands and it spread naturally via the internet to other European countries and even reached the USA. The campaigners used social utilities such as My Space and Face book to promote the message. The campaign was also promoted via its ambassadors: Scottish band Brand New Deja Vu, DJ Paul Jay and Bangladeshi writer Taslima Nasrin. GHRD made available petitions in several languages asking the Bangladeshi government to take action. The campaign was launched on 16 June 2007 with a Beach Benefit Concert at Scheveningen (Netherlands). Performances were made by Brand New Deja Vu, DJ Paul Jay, Valerius and Little Things That Kill.

PRESS CONFERENCE ON 1998 GLOBAL CAMPAIGN FOR WOMEN'S HUMAN RIGHTS

There could not be human rights without women's rights, correspondents were told this afternoon in a press conference on the 1998 Global Campaign for Women's Human Rights to demand greater attention and resources to protect and promote women's human rights.

Attending the press conference were Charlotte Bunch, Executive Director of the Center for Women's Global Leadership, Lydia Zigomo Nyatsanza of the Zimbabwe Women Lawyers' Association, Zieba Shorish Shamley of the Afghan Women's Network and Susana Fried, the Coordinator for the Campaign.

Over 250 organizations in some 80 countries were participating in the Campaign which was launched in the beginning of 1998, Ms. Bunch said. Local and regional tribunals had been held to give voice to the problems faced by women. Postcards with the message "Imagine a world where all women enjoyed their human rights" had been designed with space for messages. The Campaign had met with United Nations High Commissioner for Human Rights, Mary Robinson, and delivered all those messages to her. The messages were aimed at reminding the world that when one speaks of human rights, one is talking about the rights of women which are violated in every country of the world, Ms. Bunch said.

Fifty years after the Universal Declaration, women remained woefully unprotected by governments and the United Nations from human rights abuses. Ms. Robinson had pledged that she would accord women's human rights a priority on the human rights agenda; in particular she would look at worldwide trafficking in women and women's social and economic rights. Ms. Nyatsanza said that as part of the Campaign, the Convention on the Elimination of All Forms of Discrimination against Women had been translated into local languages and distributed to women's grassroots organizations as a way of educating women about their rights. The tribunal held in her country had looked at the ways in which women's rights concerning property, family and the workplace were violated, and had generated many articles on the subject of women's rights.

Another result was that ways in which women's human rights concerns could be incorporated into the Zimbabwe Constitution, which was currently undergoing reform, were being examined. Ms. Shamley said that in Afghanistan, women were banished from the public sphere of society. They were being denied the right to work, the right to education and access to medical care. They were sold as slaves and forced to marry. Girls as young as nine and ten were being forced to marry members of the Taliban militia, while thousands of people had been massacred by the Taliban militia because of their ethnicity and religious beliefs. Given those conditions, she said the celebration of the Universal Declaration meant nothing to the people of Afghanistan. "It's wonderful that we have the Declaration, but what is the use of rhetoric if we do not take action to protect women and children and people all over the world"? She asked. Ms. Fried said the Campaign had sought to celebrate the creative and effective work that had been done by women's human rights activists. As an example, she mentioned the fact that issues of sexual and gender violence had been incorporated into the Rome Statute. Ms. Bunch concluded by appealing for a change in the lack of political will and lack of resources devoted to the problems of women.

DEMAND WOMEN'S HUMAN RIGHTS!

On the 50th anniversary of the *Universal Declaration of Human Rights*, advocates throughout the world are calling attention to continuing violations of the human rights of women, and the urgent need for governments and intergovernmental bodies to strengthen their efforts to ensure respect for the human rights of all.

The following demands and actions seek to link efforts locally and globally through a common set of substantive concerns regarding women's human rights. These demands focus on the clear steps the *Beijing Declaration and Platform for Action* directs governments and intergovernmental organizations to take to promote and protect women's human rights. Building on the *Universal Declaration of Human Rights* and the *Vienna Declaration and Programme of Action*, the *Beijing Declaration and Platform for Action* declares: "Human rights and fundamental freedoms are the birthright of all human beings; their protection and promotion is the first responsibility of Governments" (paragraph 210). It reaffirms that "all human rights - civil, cultural, economic, political and social, including the right to development - are universal, indivisible, interdependent and interrelated, as expressed in the *Vienna Declaration and Programme of Action*...The full and equal enjoyment of all human rights and fundamental freedoms by women and girls is a priority for Governments and the United Nations and is essential for the advancement of women."

Therefore, women's human rights advocates throughout the world call upon governments and intergovernmental bodies to do the following:

Demand #1:

The *Beijing Declaration and Platform for Action* provides a detailed articulation of what implementation of the *Universal Declaration of Human Rights* means for women. Therefore, we call for increased action toward and resources for its full implementation. In order to fully achieve these goals, governments must also respect and protect defenders of the human rights of women.

- Dedicate new and expanded resources or reallocate existing resources to addressing women's human rights.
- Take immediate steps to implement the *Beijing Platform for Action*'s recommendation to fully integrate the human rights of women throughout all policies and programmes.
- Work toward ratification of the *Declaration on the Rights of Human Rights Defenders* (officially called the Draft Declaration on the Right and Responsibility of Individuals, Groups and Organs of Society to Promote and Protect Universally Recognized Human Rights and Fundamental Freedoms).

Demand #2:

Outlaw all forms of discrimination against women.

- Ensure ratification and implementation of the *Convention on the Elimination of All Forms of Discrimination Against Women (the Women's Convention)* immediately.
- Remove any reservations to the Women's Convention.
- Bring national laws and policies into compliance with the *Women's Convention.*
- Work toward adopting a strong optional protocol to the *Women's Convention* establishing a right of petition.

Demand #3:

Ensure women's right to live free from violence.

- Take concerted and systematic action to end violence against women in the home and family through all necessary means.
- Recognize that gender-based violence and discrimination, and the reprisals women experience when they resist such oppression can constitute persecution and should therefore be considered as grounds for showing a well-founded fear of persecution in refugee and asylum claims.
- Eliminate gender-based persecution in situations of war and armed conflict and provide justice and reparations to victims of such persecution.
- Work toward establishing an effective and independent International Criminal Court that includes a gender perspective throughout its statute, such as the inclusion of sexual violence and rape in the definitions of crimes against humanity and war crimes.

Demand #4:

Take steps to realize women's health, including their reproductive and sexual rights.

- Ensure the realization of women's right to the highest attainable standard of physicaland mental health.
- Secure women's access to reproductive and sexual health and rights.

Demand #5:

Secure women's economic, social and cultural rights.

- Guarantee women's right to development, by providing women with equal access to economic resources, as well as protecting their rights to own property and to equal inheritance, to land tenure and to credit and training, through law, policy and practice.
- Secure literacy for every woman and girl by ensuring equal access to education,including human rights education and legal literacy.

- Enforce women workers' rights on the basis of equality, non-discrimination and protection and to a living wage.

PROGRESS FOR WOMEN IS PROGRESS FOR ALL

UNIFEM is the women's fund at the United Nations. Established in 1976, it provides financial and technical assistance to innovative approaches aimed at fostering women's empowerment and gender equality. Today the organization's work touches the lives of women and girls in more than 100 countries. UNIFEM also helps make the voices of women heard at the United Nations - to highlight critical issues and advocate for the implementation of existing commitments made to women.

Placing the realization of women's human rights and security at the centre of all of its efforts, UNIFEM focuses its activities on four strategic goals:

i. Reducing women's poverty and exclusion;

ii. Ending violence against women;

iii. Reversing the spread of HIV/AIDS among women and girls; and

iv. Supporting women's leadership in governance and post-conflict reconstruction.

To pursue these goals, UNIFEM is active in all regions and at different levels. It works with countries to formulate and implement laws and policies to eliminate gender discrimination and promote gender equality in such areas as land and inheritance rights, decent work for women and ending violence against women. UNIFEM also aims to transform institutions to make them more accountable to gender equality and women's rights, to strengthen the capacity and voice of women's rights advocates, and to change harmful and discriminatory practices in society.

Two international agreements frame UNIFEM's work: the Beijing Platform for Action resulting from the Fourth World Conference on Women in 1995, and the Convention on the Elimination of All Forms of Discrimination Against Women

(CEDAW), known as the women's bill of rights. The spirit of these agreements has been affirmed by the Millennium Declaration and the eight Millennium Development Goals for 2015, combating poverty, hunger, disease, illiteracy and gender inequality, and building partnerships for development. In addition, Security Council resolution 1325 on women, peace and security is a crucial reference for UNIFEM's work in support of women in conflict and post-conflict situations.

REDUCING WOMEN'S POVERTY AND EXCLUSION

While globalization offers new opportunities, it has also intensified economic insecurity for many poor women. As capital moves freely across borders, these women are increasingly concentrated in insecure, unsafe and badly paid work in the informal economy or forced to join the growing "undocumented" migrant labour stream.

UNIFEM works to enhance women's economic security by strengthening their rights to land and inheritance, increasing their access to decent work, and empowering women migrant workers in both sending and receiving countries.

In Jordan, a country of destination for migrant workers, UNIFEM has worked with the Government to formulate a minimum standard contract for migrant women that is being used to monitor working conditions. Also in Jordan, UNIFEM's partnership with CISCO Systems helped shape gender-sensitive training programmes that have increased women's access to job opportunities presented by information technology. The initiative will be replicated in several Arab countries.

Women have recognized that if you want to see how governments are implementing their commitments to women, follow the money. In over 30 countries UNIFEM supports national and local initiatives to include gender perspectives in budgeting processes, and to collect and use sex-disaggregated data in public policy formulation.

ENDING VIOLENCE AGAINST WOMEN

Violence against women is the most pervasive human rights violation - whether women are subjected to domestic violence, trafficked across borders, or the victims of systematic rape in conflict zones. Studies have shown that as many as one out of three women worldwide will be beaten, coerced into sex or otherwise abused in her lifetime.

Despite great progress in laws and policies to address gender-based violence, there is a large implementation gap. Through its Trust Fund to End Violence Against Women, UNIFEM supports innovative strategies to bridge this gap - working across multiple levels and sectors simultaneously, strengthening community ownership and including men as partners. In Eastern and Southern Africa, for example, men from all walks of life spread the message against violence through music, dance and drama in rural and urban communities. In Tanzania, the Women's Judges Association received a grant to train judges and magistrates on jurisprudence and equality. And in China, a Trust Fund grant helped expand the network of support stations for domestic violence cases.

REVERSING THE SPREAD OF HIV/AIDS AMONG WOMEN AND GIRLS

HIV/AIDS increasingly has a young woman's face. Today, over 60 per cent of 15–24 year olds living with HIV/AIDS are women.

UNIFEM focuses on enhancing HIV/AIDS policies and translating them into effective strategies on the ground. The fund works with National AIDS Councils and Ministries to devise national programmes and policies that ensure women's equal access to prevention, care and treatment. In Brazil, support was rendered to an organization of Afro-Brazilian women to monitor access to HIV/AIDS-related public services.

UNIFEM also assists HIV-positive women who are advocating for a future in which they can live without stigma and violence, have easy access to drugs and continue to live healthy and meaningful lives. Support to the Positive Women's Network in India, for example, has resulted in their issues being taken up by the National Commission of Women. In addition, UNIFEM has formed a partnership with the Indian Railways - the third largest employer in the world - to reach employees with critical information on gender and HIV/AIDS through peer educators.

SUPPORTING WOMEN'S LEADERSHIP IN GOVERNANCE AND POST-CONFLICT CONSTRUCTION

Women remain vastly under-represented in national or local assemblies, accounting for a worldwide average of some 15 per cent of seats in national parliaments. When it comes to negotiating peace and facilitating reconstruction after wars, women's exclusion is even more pronounced - despite the fact that they are particularly affected and can be part of the solution.

In post-conflict situations, when electoral processes, new constitutions and legislative structures are being created, it is critical for women to be involved. UNIFEM has actively supported women in electoral and constitutional processes in a number of countries. In Afghanistan, for example, where in December 2003 the Loya Jirga enshrined equality between men and women in the nation's new Constitution. This achievement required broad-based alliances and ongoing advocacy. A UNIFEM-facilitated Gender and Law Working Group - comprised of the Office of the State Minister for Women, the Ministry of Women's Affairs (MOWA), Supreme Court judges and women's NGOs - reviewed the draft Constitution and advocated for the recognition of women as full citizens.

VIOLENCE AGAINST WOMEN: A FACT SHEET

In the US, a woman is raped every 6 minutes; a woman is battered every 15 seconds. In North Africa, 6,000 women are genitally mutilated each day. This year, more than 15,000 women will be sold into sexual slavery in China. 200 women in Bangladesh will be horribly disfigured when their spurned husbands or suitors burn them with acid. More than 7,000 women in India will be murdered by their families and in-laws in disputes over dowries. Violence against women is rooted in a global culture of discrimination which denies women equal rights with men and which legitimizes the appropriation of women's bodies for individual gratification or political ends. Every year, violence in the home and the community devastates the lives of millions of women. Stop Violence Against Women.

Violence against women is a violation of human rights that cannot be justified by any political, religious, or cultural claim. A global culture of discrimination against women allows violence to occur daily and with impunity. Amnesty International calls on you to help us eradicate violence against women and help women to achieve lives of equality and human dignity.

Violence against women feeds off discrimination and serves to reinforce it. When women are abused in custody, when they are raped by armed forces as "spoils of war", or when they are terrorized by violence in the home, unequal power relations between men and women are both manifested and enforced.

Violence against women is compounded by discrimination on the grounds of race, ethnicity, sexual identity, social status, class, and age. Such multiple forms of discrimination further restrict women's choices, increase their vulnerability to violence and make it even harder for women to obtain justice.

There is an unbroken spectrum of violence that women face at the hands of people who exert control over them. States have the obligation to prevent, protect against, and punish violence against women whether perpetrated by private or public actors. States have a responsibility to uphold standards of due diligence and take steps to fulfill their responsibility to protect individuals from human rights abuses.

INTERNATIONAL WOMEN'S HUMAN RIGHTS FOUNDATIONS

The Universal Declaration of Human Rights states that "everyone is entitled to all the rights and freedoms set forth in this Declaration, without distinction of any kind, such as race, color, sex, language, religion, political or other opinion, national or social origin, property, birth or other status." (Article 2)

The Declaration on the Elimination of Violence Against Women states that "violence against women means any act of gender-based violence that results in, or is likely to result in, physical, sexual or psychological harm or suffering to women, including threats of such acts, coercion or arbitrary deprivation of liberty, whether occurring in public or in private life." (Article 1) It further asserts that states have an obligation to " exercise due diligence to prevent, investigate and, in accordance with national legislation, punish acts of violence against women, whether those acts are perpetrated by the State or by private persons." (Article 4-c)

The Convention on the Elimination of all forms of Discrimination Against Women (CEDAW), defines discrimination against women as any "distinction, exclusion or restriction made on the basis of sex which has the effect or purpose of impairing or nullifying the recognition, enjoyment or exercise by women, irrespective of their marital status, on the basis of equality between men and women, of human rights or fundamental freedoms in the political, economic, social, cultural, civil or any other field." (Article 1)

VIOLENCE AGAINST WOMEN: A HUMAN RIGHTS VIOLATION

Violence against women is rampant in all corners of the world. Such violence is a human rights violation that manifests itself in a number of ways, including:

1. Violence against women in custody

The imbalance of power between inmates and guards is a result of prisoners' total dependency on correctional officers and guards' ability to withhold privileges and is manifest in direct physical force and indirect abuses. Because incarcerated women are largely invisible to the public eye, little is done when the punishment of imprisonment is compounded with that of rape, sexual assault, groping during body searches, and shackling during childbirth. Women are often coerced into providing sex for "favors" such as extra food or personal hygiene products, or to avoid punishment. There is little medical or psychological care available to inmates. Though crimes in prison such as rape are prevalent, few perpetrators of violence against female inmates are ever held accountable. In 1997, for example, only ten prison employees in the entire federal system were disciplined for sexual misconduct.

2. Acid Burning and Dowry Deaths

Women's subjugation to men is pervasive in the political, civil, social, cultural, and economic spheres of many countries. In such societies, a woman who turns down a suitor or does not get along with her in-laws far too frequently becomes a victim of a violent form of revenge: acid burning. Acid is thrown in her face or on her body and can blind her in addition to often fatal third-degree burns. Governments do little to prevent the sale of acid to the public or to punish those who use it to kill and maim. Similarly, the ongoing reality of dowry-related violence is an example of what can happen when women are treated as property. Brides unable to pay the high "price" to marry are punished by violence and often death at the hands of their in-laws or their own husbands.

3. Honor Killings

In some societies, women are often looked upon as representatives of the honor of the family. When women are suspected of extra-marital sexual relations, even if in the case of rape, they can be subjected to the cruelest forms of indignity and violence often by their own fathers or brothers. Women, who are raped and are unable to provide explicit evidence, are sometimes accused of zina, or the crime of unlawful sexual relations, the punishment for which is often death by public stoning. Such laws serve as a great obstacle inhibiting women from pursuing cases against those who raped them. Assuming an accused woman's guilt, male family members believe that they have no other means of undoing a perceived infringement of "honor" other than to kill the woman.

4. Domestic violence

Violence against women is a global pandemic. Without exception, a woman's greatest risk of violence is from someone she knows. Domestic violence is a violation of a woman's right to physical integrity, to liberty, and all too often, to her right to life itself. When states fail to take the basic steps needed to protect women from domestic violence or allow these crimes to be committed with impunity, states are failing in their obligation to protect women from torture.

5. Female Genital Mutilation

Female genital mutilation is the removal of part or all of the external female genitalia. In its most severe form, a woman or girl has all of her genitalia removed and then stitched together, leaving a small opening for intercourse and menstruation. It is practiced in 28 African countries on the pretext of cultural tradition or hygiene. An estimated 135 million girls have undergone FGM with dire consequences ranging from infection (including HIV) to sterility, in addition to the devastating psychological effects. Though all the governments of the countries in which FGM is practiced have legislation making it illegal, the complete lack of enforcement and prosecution of the perpetrators means FGM continues to thrive.

HUMAN RIGHTS VIOLATIONS BASED ON ACTUAL OR PERCEIVED SEXUAL IDENTITY

Sexuality is regulated in a gender specific way and maintained through strict constraints imposed by cultural norms and sometimes through particular legal measures supporting those norms. The community, which can include religious institutions, the media, family and cultural networks, regulates women's sexuality and punishes women who do not comply. Such women include lesbians, women who appear "too masculine," women who try to freely exercise their rights and women who challenge male dominance. Lesbian women, or women who are perceived to be lesbian, experience abuses by state authorities in prisons, by the police, as well as private actors such as their family and community. Numerous cases document young lesbians being beaten, raped, forcibly impregnated or married, and otherwise attacked by family members to punish them or "correct" their sexual identity. Lesbians in the United States face well-founded fears of persecution by police because of their sexual identity and violence against lesbians occurs with impunity on a regular basis.

GENDER BASED ASYLUM

The UN High Commission on Refugees advocates that "women fearing persecution or severe discrimination on the basis of their gender should be considered a member of a social group for the purposes of determining refugee status." (*Guidelines on the Protection of Refugee Women*) Such persecution may include harms unique to their gender such as, but not limited to, female genital mutilation, forcible abortion, domestic violence that the state refuses to act on and honor killings. However, women seeking asylum in the United States rarely gain refugee status based on claims of gender-related violence, as U.S. asylum adjudicators apply a restrictive interpretation of the international definition of a refugee entitled to persecution. In particular, lesbian women seeking asylum from sexuality-based persecution in their countries of origin often, and legitimately, fear disclosing their sexuality to authorities.

THE PROBLEM OF IMPUNITY

Perpetrators of violence against women are rarely held accountable for their acts. Women who are victims of gender-related violence often have little recourse because many state agencies are themselves guilty of gender bias and discriminatory practices. Many women opt not to report cases of violence to authorities because they fear being ostracized and shamed by communities that are too often quick to blame victims of violence for the abuses they have suffered. When women do challenge their abusers, it can often only be accomplished by long and humiliating court battles with little sympathy from authorities or the media. Violence against women is so deeply embedded in society that it often fails to garner public censure and outrage.

8

The Human Rights of Women

CHARTER OF THE UNITED NATIONS

We the peoples of the United Nations determined to save succeeding generations from the scourge of war, which twice in our lifetime has brought untold sorrow to mankind, and

To reaffirm faith in fundamental human rights, in the dignity and worth of the human person, in the equal rights of men and women and of nations large and small, and

To establish conditions under which justice and respect for the obligations arising from treaties and other sources of international law can be maintained

PURPOSES AND PRINCIPLES

Article 1

The Purposes of the United Nations are:

1. To maintain international peace and security.
2. To achieve international co-operation in solving international problems of an economic, social, cultural, or humanitarian character, and in promoting and encouraging respect for human rights and for fundamental freedoms for all without distinction as to race, sex, language, or religion.

Article 8

The United Nations shall place no restrictions on the eligibility of men and women to participate in any capacity and under conditions of equality in its principal and subsidiary organs.

Article 55

With a view to the creation of conditions of stability and well-being which are necessary for peaceful and friendly relations among nations based on respect for the principle of equal rights and self-determination of peoples, the United Nations shall promote:

a. Higher standards of living, full employment, and conditions of economic and social progress and development;
b. Solutions of international economic, social, health, and related problems and international cultural and educational co-operation; and
c. Universal respect for and observance of, human rights and fundamental freedoms for all without distinction as to race, sex, language, or religion.

UNIVERSAL DECLARATION OF HUMAN RIGHTS

Preamble

Whereas recognition of the inherent dignity and of the equal and inalienable rights of all members of the human family is the foundation of freedom, justice and peace in the world,

Whereas the peoples of the United Nations have in the Charter reaffirmed their faith in fundamental human rights, in the dignity and worth of the human person and in the equal rights of men and women and have determined to promote social progress and better standards of life in larger freedom.

Article 2

Everyone is entitled to all the rights and freedoms set forth in this Declaration, without distinction of any kind, such as race, colour, sex, language, religion, political or other opinion, national or social origin, property, birth or other status.

Article 7

All are equal before the law and are entitled without any discrimination to equal protection of the law. All are entitled to equal protection against any discrimination in violation of this Declaration and against any incitement to such discrimination.

Article 16

1. Men and women of full age, without any limitation due to race, nationality or religion, have the right to marry and to found a family. They are entitled to equal rights as to marriage during marriage and at its dissolution.
2. Marriage shall be entered into only with the free and full consent of the intending spouses.
3. The family is the natural and fundamental group unit of society and is entitled to protection by society and the State.

Article 25

1. Everyone has the right to a standard of living adequate for the health and well-being of himself and of his family, including food, clothing, and housing and medical care and necessary social services, and the right to security in the event of unemployment, sickness, disability, widowhood, old age or other lack of livelihood in circumstances beyond his control.
2. Motherhood and childhood are entitled to special care and assistance. All children, whether born in or out of wedlock, shall enjoy the same social protection.

INTERNATIONAL COVENANT ON ECONOMIC, SOCIAL AND CULTURAL RIGHTS

Article 2

The States Parties to the present Covenant undertake to guarantee that the rights enunciated in the present Covenant will be exercised without discrimination of any kind as to race, colour, sex, language, religion, politics or other opinion, national or social origin, property, birth or other status.

Article 3

The States Parties to the present Covenant undertake to ensure the equal right of men and women to the enjoyment of all economic, social and cultural rights set forth in the present Covenant.

Article 10

The States Parties to the present Covenant recognize that:

1. The widest possible protection and assistance should be accorded to the family, which is the natural and fundamental group unit of society, particularly for its establishment and while it is responsible for the care and educate of dependent children. Marriage must be entered into with the free consent of the intending spouses.
2. Special protection should be accorded to mothers during a reasonable period before and after childbirth. During such period working mothers should be accorded paid leave or leave with adequate social security benefits.
3. Special measures of protection and assistance should be taken on behalf of all children and young persons without any discrimination for reasons of parentage or other conditions. Children and young persons should be protected from economic and social exploitation. Their employment in work harmful to their morals or health or dangerous to life or likely to hamper their normal development should be punishable by law. States should also set age limits below which the paid employment of child labour should be prohibited and punishable by law.

Article 12

1. The States Parties to the present Covenant recognize the right of everyone to the enjoyment of the highest attainable standard of physical and mental health.
2. The steps to be taken by the States Parties to the present Covenant to achieve the full realization of this right shall include those necessary for:
   a. The provision for the reduction of the still birth-rate; and
   b. Infant mortality and for the healthy development of the child.

INTERNATIONAL COVENANT ON CIVIL AND POLITICAL RIGHTS

Article 2

1. Each State Party to the present Covenant undertakes to respect and to ensure to all individuals within its territory and subject to its jurisdiction the rights recognized in the present Covenant, without distinction of any kind, such as race, colour, sex, language, religion, politics or other opinion, national or social origin property, birth or other status.

Article 3

The States Parties to the present Covenant undertake to ensure the equal right of men and women to the enjoyment of all civil and political rights set forth in the present Covenant.

Article 14

1. All persons shall be equal before the courts and tribunals. In the determination of any criminal charge against him, or of his rights and obligations in a suit at law, everyone shall be entitled to a fair and public hearing by a compact, independent and impartial tribunal established by law. The Press and the public may be excluded from all or part of a trial for reasons of morals, public order (*ordre public*) or national security in a democratic society, or when the interest of the private lives of the parties so requires, or to the extent strictly necessary in the opinion of the court in special circumstances where publicity would prejudice the interests of justice; but any judgement rendered in a criminal case or in a suit at law shall be made public except where the interest of juvenile persons otherwise requires or the proceedings concern matrimonial disputes or the guardianship of children.

Article 16

Everyone shall have the right to recognition everywhere as a person before the law.

Article 18

1. Everyone shall have the right to freedom of thought, conscience and religion.
2. The States Parties to the present Covenant undertake to have respect for the liberty of parents and, when applicable, legal guardians to ensure the religious and moral education of their children in conformity with their own convictions.

Article 23

1. The family is the natural and fundamental group unit of society and is entitled to protection by society and the State.
2. The right of men and women of marriageable age to marry and to found a family shall be recognized.
3. No marriage shall be entered into without the free and full consent of the intending spouses.
4. States Parties to the present Covenant shall take appropriate steps to ensure equality of rights and responsibilities of spouses as to marriage during marriage and at its dissolution. In the case of dissolution, provision shall be made for the necessary protection of any children.

Article 24

1. Every child shall have, without any discrimination as to race, colour, sex, language, religion, national or social origin, property or birth, the right to such measures of protection as are required by his status as a minor, on the part of his family, society and the State.
2. Every child shall be registered immediately after birth and shall have a name.
3. Every child has the right to acquire nationality.

Article 26

All persons are equal before the law and are entitled without any discrimination to the equal protection of the law. In this respect, the law shall prohibit any discrimination and guarantee to all persons equal and effective protection against discrimination on any ground such as race, colour, sex, language, religion, political or other opinion, national or social origin, property, birth or other status.

CONVENTION ON THE RIGHTS OF THE CHILD

Preamble

The States Parties to the present Convention,

Bearing in mind that the peoples of the United Nations have, in the Charter, reaffirmed their faith in fundamental human rights and in the dignity and worth of the human person, and have determined to promote social progress and better standards of life in larger freedom,

Recognizing that the United Nations has, in the Universal Declaration of Human Rights and in the International Covenants on Human Rights, proclaimed and agreed that everyone is entitled to all the rights and freedoms set forth therein, without distinction of any kind, such as race, colour, sex, language, religion, political or other opinion, national or social origin, property, birth or other status,

Recalling that, in the Universal Declaration of Human Rights, the United Nations has proclaimed that childhood is entitled to special care and assistance,

Recalling the provisions of the Declaration on Social and Legal Principles relating to the Protection and Welfare of Children, with Special Reference to Foster Placement and Adoption Nationally and Internationally; the United Nations Standard Minimum Rules for the Administration of Juvenile Justice (The Beijing Rules); and the Declaration on the Protection of Women and Children in Emergency and Armed Conflict.

Article 1

For the purposes of the present Convention, a child means every human being below the age of eighteen years unless, under the law applicable to the child, majority is attained earlier.

Article 2

1. States Parties shall respect and ensure the rights set forth in the present Convention to each child within their jurisdiction without discrimination of any kind, irrespective of the child's or his or her parent's or legal guardian's race, colour, sex, language, religion, political or other opinion, national, ethnic or social origin, property, disability, birth or other status.
2. States Parties shall take all appropriate measures to ensure that the child is protected against all forms of discrimination or punishment on the basis of the status, activities, expressed opinions, or beliefs of the child's parents, legal guardians, or family members.

Article 24

1. States Parties recognize the right of the child to the enjoyment of the highest attainable standard of health and to facilities for the treatment of illness and rehabilitation of health. States Parties shall strive to ensure that no child is deprived of his or her right of access to health care services.
2. States Parties shall pursue full implementation of this right and, in particular, shall take appropriate measures:
   a. To diminish infant and child mortality;
   b. To ensure the provision of necessary medical assistance and health care to all children with emphasis on the development of primary health care;
   c. To combat disease and malnutrition, including within the framework of primary health care, through, inter alia, the application of readily available technology and through the provision of adequate nutritious foods and clean drinking-water, taking into consideration the dangers and risks of environmental pollution;
   d. To ensure appropriate pre-natal and post-natal health care for mothers;

Article 29

1. States Parties agree that the education of the child shall be directed to:
   a. The preparation of the child for responsible life in a free society, in the spirit of understanding, peace, tolerance, equality of sexes, and friendship among all peoples, ethnic, national and religious groups and persons of indigenous origin.

CONVENTION ON THE ELIMINATION OF ALL FORMS OF DISCRIMINATION AGAINST WOMEN

Adopted and opened for signature, ratification and accession by General Assembly resolution 34/180 of 18 December 1979

Entered into force: 3 September 1981, in accordance with article 27 (1)

The States Parties to the present Convention,

Noting that the Charter of the United Nations reaffirms faith in fundamental human rights, in the dignity and worth of the human person and in the equal rights of men and women,

Noting that the Universal Declaration of Human Rights affirms the principle of the inadmissibility of discrimination and proclaims that all human beings are born free and equal in dignity and rights and that everyone is entitled to all the rights and freedoms set forth therein, without distinction of any kind, including distinction based on sex,

Noting that the States Parties to the International Covenants on Human Rights have the obligation to ensure the equal rights of men and women to enjoy all economic, social, cultural, civil and political rights,

Considering the international conventions concluded under the auspices of the United Nations and the specialized agencies promoting equality of rights of men and women,

Noting also the resolutions, declarations and recommendations adopted by the United Nations and the specialized agencies promoting equality of rights of men and women,

Concerned, however, that despite these various instruments, extensive discrimination against women continues to exist,

Recalling that discrimination against women violates the principles of equality of rights and respect for human dignity, is an obstacle to the participation of women, on equal terms with men, in the political, social, economic and cultural life of their countries, hampers the growth of the prosperity of society and the family and makes more difficult the full development of the potentialities of women in the service of their countries and of humanity,

Concerned that in situations of poverty women have the least access to food, health, education, training and opportunities for employment and other needs,

Convinced that the establishment of the new international economic order based on equity and justice will contribute significantly towards the promotion of equality between men and women,

Emphasizing that the eradication of apartheid, all forms of racism, racial discrimination, colonialism, neocolonialism, aggression, foreign occupation and domination and interference in the internal affairs of States is essential to the full enjoyment of the rights of men and women,

Affirming that the strengthening of international peace and security, the relaxation of international tension, mutual cooperation among all States irrespective of their social and economic systems, general and complete disarmament, in particular nuclear disarmament under strict and effective international control, the affirmation of the principles of justice, equality and mutual benefit in relations among countries and the realization of the right of peoples under alien and colonial domination and foreign occupation to self determination and independence, as well as respect for national sovereignty and territorial integrity, will promote social progress and development and as a consequence will contribute to the attainment of full equality between men and women,

Convinced that the full and complete development of a country, the welfare of the world and the cause of peace require the maximum participation of women on equal terms with men in all fields,

Bearing in mind the great contribution of women to the welfare of the family and to the development of society, so far not fully recognized, the social significance of maternity and the role of both parents in the family and in the upbringing of children, and aware that the role of women in procreation should not be a basis for discrimination but that the upbringing of children requires a sharing of responsibility between men and women and society as a whole,

Aware that a change in the traditional role of men as well as the role of women in society and in the family is needed to achieve full equality between men and women,

Determined to implement the principles set forth in the Declaration on the Elimination of Discrimination against Women and, for that purpose to adopt the measures required for the elimination of such discrimination in all its forms and manifestations.

Have agreed on the following:

PART I

Article 1

For the purposes of the present Convention, the term "discrimination against women" shall mean any distinction, exclusion or restriction made on the basis of sex which has the effect or purpose of impairing or nullifying the recognition, enjoyment or exercise by women, irrespective of their marital status, on a basis of equality of men and women, of human rights and fundamental freedoms in the political, economic, social, cultural, civil or any other field.

Article 2

States Parties condemn discrimination against women in all its forms, agree to pursue by all appropriate means and without delay a policy of eliminating discrimination against women and, to this end, undertake:

a. To embody the principle of the equality of men and women in their national constitutions or other appropriate legislation if not yet incorporated therein and to ensure, through law and other appropriate means, the practical realization of this principle;
b. To adopt appropriate legislative and other measures, including sanctions where appropriate, prohibiting all discrimination against women;
c. To establish legal protection of the rights of women on an equal basis with men and to ensure through competent national tribunals and other public institutions the effective protection of women against any act of discrimination;
d. To refrain from engaging in any act or practice of discrimination against women and to ensure that public authorities and institutions shall act in conformity with this obligation;
e. To take all appropriate measures to eliminate discrimination against women by any person, organization or enterprise;
f. To take all appropriate measures, including legislation, to modify or abolish existing laws, regulations, customs and practices which constitute discrimination against women;
g. To repeal all national penal provisions which constitute discrimination against women.

Article 3

States Parties shall take in all fields, in particular in the political, social, economic and cultural fields, all appropriate measures, including legislation, to ensure the full development and advancement of women, for the purpose of guaranteeing them the exercise and enjoyment of human rights and fundamental freedoms on a basis of equality with men.

Article 4

1. Adoption by States Parties of temporary special measures aimed at accelerating de facto equality between men and women shall not be considered discrimination as defined in the present Convention, but shall in no way entail as a consequence the maintenance of unequal or separate standards; these measures shall be discontinued when the objectives of equality of opportunity and treatment have been achieved.
2. Adoption by States Parties of special measures, including those measures contained in the present Convention, aimed at protecting maternity shall not be considered discriminatory.

Article 5

States Parties shall take all appropriate measures:

a. To modify the social and cultural patterns of conduct of men and women, with a view to achieving the elimination of prejudices and customary and all other practices which are based on the idea of the inferiority or the superiority of either of the sexes or on stereotyped roles for men and women;

b. To ensure that family education includes a proper understanding of maternity as a social function and the recognition of the common responsibility of men and women in the upbringing and development of their children, it being understood that the interest of the children is the primordial consideration in all cases.

Article 6

States Parties shall take all appropriate measures, including legislation, to suppress all forms of traffic in women and exploitation of prostitution of women.

PART II

Article 7

States Parties shall take all appropriate measures to eliminate discrimination against women in the political and public life of the country and, in particular, shall ensure to women, on equal terms with men, the right:

a. To vote in all elections and public referenda and to be eligible for election to all publicly elected bodies;
b. To participate in the formulation of government policy and the implementation thereof and to hold public office and perform all public functions at all levels of government;
c. To participate in non-governmental organizations and associations concerned with the public and political life of the country.

Article 8

States Parties shall take all appropriate measures to ensure to women, on equal terms with men and without any discrimination, the opportunity to represent their Governments at the international level and to participate in the work of international organizations.

Article 9

1. States Parties shall grant women equal rights with men to acquire, change or retain their nationality. They shall ensure in particular that neither marriage to an alien nor change of nationality by the husband during marriage shall automatically change the nationality of the wife, render her stateless or force upon her the nationality of the husband.
2. States Parties shall grant women equal rights with men with respect to the nationality of their children.

PART III

Article 10

States Parties shall take all appropriate measures to eliminate discrimination against women in order to ensure to them equal rights with men in the field of education and in particular to ensure, on a basis of equality of men and women:

a. The same conditions for career and vocational guidance, for access to studies and for the achievement of diplomas in educational establishments of all categories in rural as well as in urban areas; this equality shall be ensured in preschool, general, technical, professional and higher technical education, as well as in all types of vocational training;

b. Access to the same curricula, the same examinations, teaching staff with qualifications of the same standard and school premises and equipment of the same quality;
c. The elimination of any stereotyped concept of the roles of men and women at all levels and in all forms of education by encouraging coeducation and other types of education which will help to achieve this aim and, in particular, by the revision of textbooks and school programmes and the adaptation of teaching methods;
d. The same opportunities to benefit from scholarships and other study grants;
e. The same opportunities for access to programmes of continuing education, including adult and functional literacy programmes, particularly those aimed at reducing, at the earliest possible time, any gap in education existing between men and women;
f. The reduction of female student drop-out rates and the organization of programmes for girls and women who have left school prematurely;
g. The same opportunities to participate actively in sports and physical education;
h. Access to specific educational information to help to ensure the health and well-being of families, including information and advice on family planning.

Article 11

1. States Parties shall take all appropriate measures to eliminate discrimination against women in the field of employment in order to ensure, on a basis of equality of men and women, the same rights, in particular:
   a. The right to work as an inalienable right of all human beings;

b. The right to the same employment opportunities, including the application of the same criteria for selection in matters of employment;

c. The right to free choice of profession and employment, the right to promotion, job security and all benefits and conditions of service and the right to receive vocational training and retraining, including apprenticeships, advanced vocational training and recurrent training;

d. The right to equal remuneration, including benefits, and to equal treatment in respect of work of equal value, as well as equality of treatment in the evaluation of the quality of work;

e. The right to social security, particularly in cases of retirement, unemployment, sickness, invalidity and old age and other incapacity to work, as well as the right to paid leave;

f. The right to protection of health and to safety in working conditions, including the safeguarding of the function of reproduction.

2. In order to prevent discrimination against women on the grounds of marriage or maternity and to ensure their effective right to work, States Parties shall take appropriate measures:

a. To prohibit, subject to the imposition of sanctions, dismissal on the grounds of pregnancy or of maternity leave and discrimination in dismissals on the basis of marital status.

b. To introduce maternity leave with pay or with comparable social benefits without loss of former employment, seniority or social allowances.

c. To encourage the provision of the necessary supporting social services to enable parents to combine family obligations with work responsibilities and participation in public life, in particular through promoting the establishment and development of a network of child-care facilities.

d. To provide special protection to women during pregnancy in types of work proved to be harmful to them.

3. Protective legislation relating to matters covered in this article shall be reviewed periodically in the light of scientific and technological knowledge and shall be revised, repealed or extended as necessary.

Article 12

1. States Parties shall take all appropriate measures to eliminate discrimination against women in the field of health care in order to ensure, on a basis of equality of men and women, access to health care services, including those related to family planning.
2. Notwithstanding the provisions of paragraph 1 of this article, States Parties shall ensure to women appropriate services in connection with pregnancy, confinement and the post-natal period, granting free services where necessary, as well as adequate nutrition during pregnancy and lactation.

Article 13

States Parties shall take all appropriate measures to eliminate discrimination against women in other areas of economic and social life in order to ensure, on a basis of equality of men and women, the same rights, in particular:

a. The right to family benefits;
b. The right to bank loans, mortgages and other forms of financial credit;
c. The right to participate in recreational activities, sports and all aspects of cultural life.

Article 14

1. States Parties shall take into account the particular problems faced by rural women and the significant roles which rural women play in the economic survival of their families, including their work in the non-monetized sectors of the economy, and shall take all appropriate measures to ensure the application of the provisions of the present Convention to women in rural areas.

2. States Parties shall take all appropriate measures to eliminate discrimination against women in rural areas in order to ensure, on a basis of equality of men and women, that they participate in and benefit from rural development and, in particular, shall ensure to such women the right:
    a. To participate in the elaboration and implementation of development planning at all levels;
    b. To have access to adequate health-care facilities, including information, counselling and services in family planning;
    c. To benefit directly from social security programmes;
    d. To obtain all types of training and education, formal and non-formal, including that relating to functional literacy, as well as, inter alia, the benefit of all community and extension services, in order to increase their technical proficiency;
    e. To organize self-help groups and coöperatives in order to obtain equal access to economic opportunities through employment or self-employment;
    f. To participate in all community activities;
    g. To have access to agricultural credit and loans, marketing facilities, appropriate technology and equal treatment in land and agrarian reform as well as in land resettlement schemes;
    h. To enjoy adequate living conditions, particularly in relation to housing, sanitation, electricity and water supply, transport and communications.

PART IV

Article 15

1. States Parties shall accord to women equality with men before the law.
2. States Parties shall accord to women, in civil matters, a legal capacity identical to that of men and the same opportunities to exercise that capacity. In particular, they

shall give women equal rights to conclude contracts and to administer property and shall treat them equally in all stages of procedure in courts and tribunals.

3. States Parties agree that all contracts and all other private instruments of any kind with a legal effect which is directed at restricting the legal capacity of women shall be deemed null and void.
4. States Parties shall accord to men and women the same rights with regard to the law relating to the movement of persons and the freedom to choose their residence and domicile.

Article 16

1. States Parties shall take all appropriate measures to eliminate discrimination against women in all matters relating to marriage and family relations and in particular shall ensure, on a basis of equality of men and women:
   a. The same right to enter into marriage;
   b. The same right freely to choose a spouse and to enter into marriage only with their free and full consent;
   c. The same rights and responsibilities during marriage and at its dissolution;
   d. The same rights and responsibilities as parents, irrespective of their marital status, in matters relating to their children; in all cases the interests of the children shall be paramount;
   e. The same rights to decide freely and responsibly on the number and spacing of their children and to have access to the information, education and means to enable them to exercise these rights;
   f. The same rights and responsibilities with regard to guardianship, wardship, trusteeship and adoption of children, or similar institutions where these concepts exist in national legislation; in all cases the interests of the children shall be paramount;
   g. The same personal rights as husband and wife, including the right to choose a family name, a profession and an occupation;

h. The same rights for both spouses in respect of the ownership, acquisition, management, administration, enjoyment and disposition of property, whether free of charge or for a valuable consideration.

2. The betrothal and the marriage of a child shall have no legal effect, and all necessary action, including legislation, shall be taken to specify a minimum age for marriage and to make the registration of marriages in an official registry compulsory.

PART V

Article 17

1. For the purpose of considering the progress made in the implementation of the present Convention, there shall be established a Committee on the Elimination of Discrimination against Women (hereinafter referred to as the Committee) consisting, at the time of entry into force of the Convention, of eighteen and, after ratification of or accession to the Convention by the thirty fifth State Party, of twenty-three experts of high moral standing and competence in the field covered by the Convention. The experts shall be elected by States Parties from among their nationals and shall serve in their personal capacity, consideration being given to equitable geographical distribution and to the representation of the different forms of civilization as well as the principal legal systems.
2. The members of the Committee shall be elected by secret ballot from a list of persons nominated by States Parties. Each State Party may nominate one person from among its own nationals.
3. The initial election shall be held six months after the date of the entry into force of the present Convention. At least three months before the date of each election the Secretary-General of the United Nations shall address a letter to the States Parties inviting them to submit their nominations within two months. The Secretary-General shall prepare a list in alphabetical order of all persons

thus nominated, indicating the States Parties which have nominated them, and shall submit it to the States Parties.

4. Elections of the members of the Committee shall be held at a meeting of States Parties convened by the Secretary-General at United Nations Headquarters. At that meeting, for which two thirds of the States Parties shall constitute a quorum, the persons elected to the Committee shall be those nominees who obtain the largest number of votes and an absolute majority of the votes of the representatives of States Parties present and voting.
5. The members of the Committee shall be elected for a term of four years. However, the terms of nine of the members elected at the first election shall expire at the end of two years; immediately after the first election the names of these nine members shall be chosen by lot by the Chairman of the Committee.
6. The election of the five additional members of the Committee shall be held in accordance with the provisions of paragraphs 2, 3 and 4 of this article, following the thirty-fifth ratification or accession. The terms of two of the additional members elected on this occasion shall expire at the end of two years, the names of these two members having been chosen by lot by the Chairman of the Committee.
7. For the filling of casual vacancies, the State Party whose expert has ceased to function as a member of the Committee shall appoint another expert from among its nationals, subject to the approval of the Committee.
8. The members of the Committee shall, with the approval of the General Assembly, receive emoluments from United Nations resources on such terms and conditions as the Assembly may decide, having regard to the importance of the Committee's responsibilities.
9. The Secretary-General of the United Nations shall provide the necessary staff and facilities for the effective performance of the functions of the Committee under the present Convention.

Article 18

1. States Parties undertake to submit to the Secretary-General of the United Nations, for consideration by the Committee, a report on the legislative, judicial, administrative or other measures which they have adopted to give effect to the provisions of the present Convention and on the progress made in this respect:
   a. Within one year after the entry into force for the State concerned;
   b. Thereafter at least every four years and further whenever the Committee so requests.
2. Reports may indicate factors and difficulties affecting the degree of fulfillment of obligations under the present Convention.

Article 19

1. The Committee shall adopt its own rules of procedure.
2. The Committee shall elect its officers for a term of two years.

Article 20

1. The Committee shall normally meet for a period of not more than two weeks annually in order to consider the reports submitted in accordance with article 18 of the present Convention.
2. The meetings of the Committee shall normally be held at United Nations Headquarters or at any other convenient place as determined by the Committee.

Article 21

1. The Committee shall, through the Economic and Social Council, report annually to the General Assembly of the United Nations on its activities and may make suggestions and general recommendations based on the examination of reports and information received from the States Parties. Such suggestions and general recommendations shall be included in the report of the Committee together with comments, if any, from States Parties.

2. The Secretary-General of the United Nations shall transmit the reports of the Committee to the Commission on the Status of Women for its information.

Article 22

The specialized agencies shall be entitled to be represented at the consideration of the implementation of such provisions of the present Convention as fall within the scope of their activities. The Committee may invite the specialized agencies to submit reports on the implementation of the Convention in areas falling within the scope of their activities.

PART VI

Article 23

Nothing in the present Convention shall affect any provisions that are more conducive to the achievement of equality between men and women which may be contained:

a. In the legislation of a State Party; or
b. In any other international convention, treaty or agreement in force for that State.

Article 24

State Parties undertake to adopt all necessary measures at the national level aimed at achieving the full realization of the rights recognized in the present Convention.

Article 25

1. The present Convention shall be open for signature by all States.
2. The Secretary-General of the United Nations is designated as the depositary of the present Convention.
3. The present Convention is subject to ratification. Instruments of ratification shall be deposited with the Secretary-General of the United Nations.
4. The present Convention shall be open to accession by all States. Accession shall be effected by the deposit of an instrument of accession with the Secretary General of the United Nations.

Article 26

1. A request for the revision of the present Convention may be made at any time by any State Party by means of a notification in writing addressed to the Secretary-General of the United Nations.
2. The General Assembly of the United Nations shall decide upon the steps, if any, to be taken in respect of such a request.

Article 27

1. The present Convention shall enter into force on the thirtieth day after the date of deposit with the Secretary-General of the United Nations of the twentieth instrument of ratification or accession.
2. For each State ratifying the present Convention or acceding to it after the deposit of the twentieth instrument of ratification or accession, the Convention shall enter into force on the thirtieth day after the date of the deposit of its own instrument of ratification or accession.

Article 28

1. The Secretary-General of the United Nations shall receive and circulate to all States the text of reservations made by States at the time of ratification or accession.
2. A reservation incompatible with the object and purpose of the present Convention shall not be permitted.
3. Reservations may be withdrawn at any time by notification to this effect addressed to the Secretary-General of the United Nations, who shall then inform all States thereof. Such notification shall take effect on the date on which it is received.

Article 29

1. Any dispute between two or more States Parties concerning the interpretation or application of the present Convention which is not settled by negotiation shall, at the request of one of them, be submitted to arbitration. If within six months from the date of the request for arbitration the parties are unable to agree on the

organization of the arbitration, any one of those parties may refer the dispute to the International Court of Justice by request in conformity with the Statute of the Court.

2. Each State Party may at the time of signature or ratification of the present Convention or accession thereto declare that it does not consider itself bound by paragraph 1 of this article. The other States Parties shall not be bound by that paragraph with respect to any State Party which has made such a reservation.
3. Any State Party which has made a reservation in accordance with paragraph 2 of this article may at any time withdraw that reservation by notification to the Secretary-General of the United Nations.

Article 30

The present Convention, the Arabic, Chinese, English, French, Russian and Spanish texts of which are equally authentic, shall be deposited with the Secretary-General of the United Nations.

IN WITNESS WHEREOF the undersigned, duly authorized, have signed the present Convention.

DECLARATION ON THE ELIMINATION OF VIOLENCE AGAINST WOMEN

Resolution adopted by the General Assembly on the report of the Third Committee

(A/48/629) Resolution 48/104

The General Assembly,

Recognizing the urgent need for the universal application to women of the rights and principles with regard to equality, security, liberty, integrity and dignity of all human beings,

Noting that those rights and principles are enshrined in international instruments, including the Universal Declaration of Human Rights, the International Covenant on Civil and Political Rights, the International Covenant on Economic, Social and Cultural Rights, the Convention on the Elimination of All Forms of Discrimination against Women and the

Convention against Torture and Other Cruel, Inhuman or Degrading Treatment or Punishment,

Recognizing that effective implementation of the Convention on the Elimination of All Forms of Discrimination against Women would contribute to the elimination of violence against women end that the Declaration on the Elimination of Violence against Women, set forth in the present resolution, will strengthen and complement that process,

Concerned that violence against women is an obstacle to the achievement of equality, development and peace, as recognized in the Nairobi Forward-looking Strategies for the Advancement of Women, in which a set of measures to combat violence against women was recommended, and to the full implementation of the Convention on the Elimination of All Forms of Discrimination against Women,

Affirming that violence against women constitutes a violation of the rights and fundamental freedoms of women and impairs or nullifies their enjoyment of those rights and freedoms, and concerned about the long-standing failure to protect and promote chose rights and freedoms in the case of violence against women,

Recognizing that violence against women is a manifestation of historically unequal power relations between men and women, which have led to domination over and discrimination against women by men and to the prevention of the full advancement of women, and that violence against women is one of the crucial social mechanisms by which women are forced into a subordinate position compared with men,

Concerned that some groups of women, such as women belonging to minority groups, indigenous women, refugee women, migrant women, women living in rural or remote communities, destitute women, women in institutions or in detention, female children, women with disabilities, elderly women and women in situations of armed conflict, are especially vulnerable to violence,

Recalling the conclusion in paragraph 23 of the annex to Economic and Social Council resolution 1990/15 of 24 May 1990 that the recognition that violence against women in the family and society was pervasive and cut across lines of income, class and culture had to be matched by urgent and effective steps to eliminate its incidence,

Recalling also Economic and Social Council resolution 1991/18 of 30 May 1991, in which the Council recommended the development of a framework for an international instrument that, would address explicitly the issue of violence against women,

Welcoming the role that women's movements are playing in drawing increasing attention to the nature, severity and magnitude of the problem of violence against women,

Alarmed that opportunity for women to achieve legal, social, political and economic equality in society are limited, *inter alia*, by continuing and endemic violence,

Convinced that in the light of the above there is a need for a clear and comprehensive definition of violence against women, a clear statement of the rights to be applied to ensure the elimination of violence against women in all its forms, a commitment by States in respect of their responsibilities, and a commitment by the international community at large to the elimination of violence against women,

Solemnly proclaims the following Declaration on the Elimination of Violence against Women and urges that every effort be made so that it becomes generally known and respected:

Article 1

For the purposes of this Declaration, the term "violence against women" means any act of gender-based violence that results in, or is likely to result in, physical, sexual or psychological harm or suffering to women, including threats of such acts, coercion or arbitrary deprivation of liberty, whether occurring in public or in private life.

Article 2

Violence against women shall be understood to encompass, but not be limited to, the following:

a. Physical, sexual and psychological violence occurring in the family, including battering, sexual abuse of female children in the household, dowry related violence, marital rape, female genital mutilation and other traditional practices harmful to women, non-spousal violence, and violence related to exploitation;

b. Physical, sexual and psychological violence occurring within the general community, including rape, sexual abuse, sexual harassment, and intimidation at work, in educational institutions and elsewhere, trafficking in women and forced prostitution;

c. Physical, sexual and psychological violence perpetuated or condoned by the State, wherever it occurs.

Article 3

Women are entitled to the equal enjoyment and protection of all human rights and fundamental freedoms in the political, economic, social, cultural, civil, or any other field. Theses rights include, *inter alia:*

a. The right to life;

b. The right to equality;

c. The right to liberty and security of person;

d. The right to equal protection under the law;

e. The right to be free from all forms of discrimination;

f. The right to the highest standard attainable of physical and mental health;

g. The right to just and favorable conditions of work;

h. The right not to be subjected to torture, or other cruel, inhuman or degrading treatment or punishment.

Article 4

States should condemn violence against women and

should not invoke any custom, tradition, or religious consideration to avoid their obligations with respect to its elimination. States should pursue by all appropriate means and without delay a policy of eliminating violence against women and, to this end, should:

a. Consider, where they have not yet done so, ratifying or acceding to the Convention on the Elimination of All Forms of Discrimination Against Women or withdrawing reservations to that Convention;
b. Refrain from engaging in violence against women;
c. Exercise due diligence to prevent, investigate and, in accordance with national legislation, punish acts of violence against women, whether those acts are perpetrated by the State or by private persons;
d. Develop penal, civil, labour and administrative sanctions in domestic legislation to punish and redress the wrongs caused to women who are subjected to violence: women who are subjected to violence should be provided with access to the mechanisms of justice and, as provided for by national legislation, to just and effective remedies to the harm they have suffered; States should also inform women of their rights in seeking redress through mechanisms;
e. Consider the possibility of developing national plans of action to promote the protection of women against any form of violence, or to include provisions for that purpose in plans already existing, taking into account, as appropriate, such cooperation as can be provided by non-governmental organizations, particularly those concerned with the issue of violence against women;
f. Develop, in a comprehensive way, preventative approaches and all those measures of legal, political, administrative and cultural nature that promote the protection of women against any form of violence, and ensure that the re victimization of women does not occur because of laws insensitive to gender considerations, enforcement practices or other interventions;

g. Work to ensure, to the maximum extent feasible in the light of their available resources and, where needed, within the framework of international cooperation, that women subjected to violence and, where appropriate, their children have specialized assistance, such as rehabilitation, assistance in child care and maintenance, treatment, counselling, and health and social services, facilities and programmes, as well as support structures, and should take all other appropriate measures to promote their safety and physical and psychological rehabilitation;
h. Include in government budgets adequate resources for their activities related to the elimination of violence against women;
i. Take measures to ensure that law enforcement officers and public officials responsible for implementing policies to prevent, investigate and punish violence against women receive training to sensitize them to the needs of women;
j. Adopt all appropriate measures, especially in the field of education, to modify the social and cultural patterns of conduct of men and women to eliminate prejudices, customary practices and all other practices based on the idea of inferiority or superiority of either of the sexes and on stereotyped roles for men and women;
k. Promote research, collect data and compile statistics, especially concerning domestic violence, relating to the prevalence of different forms of violence against women and encourage research on the causes, nature, seriousness and consequences of violence against women and on the effectiveness of measures implemented to prevent and redress violence against women; those statistics and findings of the research will be made public;
l. Adopt measures directed towards the elimination of violence against women who are especially vulnerable to violence;
m. Include, in submitting reports as required under relevant human rights instruments of the United Nations,

information pertaining to violence against women and measures taken to implement the present Declaration;

n. Encourage the development of appropriate guidelines to assist in the implementation of the principles set forth in the present Declaration;

o. Recognize the important role of the women's movement and non-governmental organizations world wide in raising awareness and alleviating the problem of violence against women;

p. Facilitate and enhance the work of the women's movement and non-governmental organizations and cooperate with them at local, national and regional levels;

q. Encourage intergovernmental regional organizations of which they are members to include the elimination of violence against women in their programmes, as appropriate.

Article 5

The organs and specialized agencies of the United Nations system should, within their respective fields of competence, contribute to the recognition and realization of the rights and the principles set forth in the present Declaration and, to this end, should, inter alia:

a. Foster international and regional cooperation with a view to defining regional strategies for combating violence, exchanging experiences and financing programmes relating to the elimination of violence against women;

b. Promote meetings and seminars with the aim of creating and raising awareness among all persons of the issue of the elimination of violence against women;

c. Foster coordination and exchange within the United Nations system between human rights treaty bodies to address the issue of violence against women effectively;

d. Include in analyses prepared by organizations and bodies of the United Nations system of social trends and problems, such as the periodic reports on the world social situation, examination of trends in violence against women;

e. Encourage coordination between organizations and bodies of the United Nations system to incorporate the issue of violence against women into ongoing programmes, especially with reference to groups of women particularly vulnerable to violence;

f. Promote the formulation of guidelines or manuals relating to violence against women, taking into account the measures referred to in the present Declaration;

g. Consider the issue of the elimination of violence against women, as appropriate, in fulfilling their mandates with respect to the implementation of human rights instruments;

h. Cooperate with non-governmental organizations in addressing the issue of violence against women.

Article 6

Nothing in the present Declaration shall affect any provision that is more conducive to the elimination of violence against women that may be contained in the legislation of a State or in any international convention, treaty or other instrument in force in a State.

SPECIAL RAPPORTEUR ON VIOLENCE AGAINST WOMEN CONCLUDES MISSION TO ALGERIA

The Algerian Constitution provides for non-discrimination between men and women and requires the state to actively ensure equality of rights and duties of all citizens, men and women alike.

Algeria has distinguished itself by realizing the equal access of boys and girls to all levels of education in little more than one generation. Today, girls are numerically overrepresented in secondary schools, colleges and universities. This is most commendable and it will help to eventually eliminate the high levels of female illiteracy inherited from colonial rule.

Educated urban women have also achieved impressive levels of representation in key areas of the public sector, especially among judges, medical doctors and teachers. Overall, however, women are particularly underrepresented among decision-makers in the private sector, the administration and politics. Women's equal access to paid work remains a problem, especially for rural and less educated women. Furthermore, in a resource-rich country like Algeria, poverty is all too visible and it has a distinct female face. Poor women, who are single mothers, deserted or divorced women or girls born out-of-wedlock are particularly burdened and they need more support and protection from the State.

A presidential decree from 2005, confirmed by both chambers of Parliament, has successfully established the equality of men and women under the Nationality Code. Significant reforms of the Family Code of 1984 have also been enacted into law. However, in family matters and access to property women still face discrimination. While the reform has removed some of the critical areas of inequality for women, it falls short of responding to the needs and aspirations of Algerian women.

Women's unequal access to inheritance creates particular vulnerabilities for them. In the event of a divorce, only women with children are entitled to the marital home or equivalent accommodation, which they often lose along with the custody of their children, should they remarry. The Family Law stipulates the strict separation of property between husband and wife. In case of divorce, however, the major assets acquired during marriage are typically assumed to belong only to the husband leaving divorced women in destitution. These are some major areas of concern that discriminate against women and seem not in line with the Algerian Constitution and they violate Algeria's international legal obligations. Reforms must continue to ensure women's autonomy and equal access to housing and sources of livelihood.

Recent surveys reveal that violence against women is a major concern in Algeria in both the home and the public space. However, this serious human rights concern remains largely invisible. The social taboos around violence in the society and the lack of a sufficient institutional response and support for victims of violence silence the victims and perpetuate the violence. During my mission, I also spoke with a number of girls and women, who had experienced violence from their husbands or other family members and had been ejected from their homes. Having to live in the streets, these women encounter multiple forms of violence.

In the work place, women experience sexual harassment by superiors and colleagues. The Government has recently criminalized certain forms of sexual harassment, which is a positive first step towards addressing this problem. The National Strategy to Combat Violence against Women, which has been prepared by the Minister-Delegate for Family and the Status of Women in consultation with other stakeholders. Provided that this promising initiative is adopted by the Cabinet, it will mark a first step of a long process that requires close partnership between relevant Ministries, the United Nations and non-governmental associations for women's rights. Ultimately, the Government will have to be measured against the concrete measures it takes to combat violence and gender inequality it is embedded in.

Women also still suffer from the legacy of the Black Decade of violence, which has seen systematic and widespread rape and sexual enslavement of women. In September 2005, Algeria adopted by way of public referendum a National Charter on Peace and Reconciliation. The National Charter foresees penal and civil amnesty for crimes committed during the decade of violence, including grave human rights violations such as acts of torture and enforced disappearances.

It is positive to note that according to the National Charter, all persons implicated in rape, collective massacres and bombings in public places - serious crimes that affected women disproportionately - have been specifically exempted from enjoying amnesty. At this stage, however, it remains most unclear to what extent the exemption clause has been applied to individual cases and also concerned about a provision in the Decree implementing the National Charter, which criminalizes the use or exploitation of the wounds of the national tragedy to harm the state, its institutions, agents or international image. Although it seems that no one has yet been prosecuted under this provision, this ambiguous norm may pose a severe obstacle to the enjoyment of the right to freedom of expression.

Persons with divergent views on how to achieve national reconciliation, including human rights defenders, victims of terrorist violence and families of disappeared persons, must be able to express themselves freely and not be subjected to harassment and threats.

The National Charter makes provision for compensation. However, wives and mothers of disappeared, who have suffered emotional violence during years of uncertainty about the fate of close family members, still report bureaucratic obstacles and delays in attaining such compensation. Questions also remain as to whether and how victims of rape and sexual enslavement during the Black Decade are to receive compensation.

Algerian women have played key roles in the most crucial stages of the history of the Democratic People's Republic. Women took an active role in the war of liberation from French colonial domination. During the Black Decade, many Algerian women displayed acts of civil courage by defying terrorist intimidation and risking terrorist violence day after day. I would also like to acknowledge the invaluable work undertaken by women today - individually and as members of voluntary associations - for the promotion and protection of women's rights. Algeria's women deserve the country's full support in their struggle to fully achieve their equality and human rights.

Bibliography

Alfred M. de Zayas, The Follow-Up Procedure of the UN Human Rights Committee, 1991 Int'l. Commission Jurists Rev. 28 (1991).

Amnesty International USA, The Universal Declaration of Human Rights, 1948-1988: Human Rights, The United Nations, and Amnesty International, New York: Amnesty International USA, 1988.

Ann Marie Clark, Strong Principles, Strengthening Practices: Amnesty International and Three Cases of Change in International Human Rights Standards, 1995 (unpublished Ph.D. thesis, University of Minnesota).

Asbjorn Eide, Pocket Guide to the Development of Human Rights Institutions and Mechanisms, Strasbourg: Council of Europe, 1989.

Conference on Security and Cooperation in Europe: An Overview of the CSCE Process, Recent Meetings and Institutional Development, Washington, D.C.: Commission on Security and Cooperation in Europe, 1992.

Diana Vincent-Daviss, Human Rights Law: A Research Guide to the Literature—Part I: International Law and the United Nations, 14 N.Y.U.J. Int'l L. & Pol. 209-319 (1981).

Diana Vincent-Daviss, Human Rights Law: A Research Guide to the Literature—Part II: International Protection of Refugees and Humanitarian Law, 14 N.Y.U.J. Int'l L. & Pol. 487-573 (1982).

Dominic McGoldrick, The Human Rights Committee, Oxford: Clarendon; New York: Oxford University Press, 1991.

Economic, Social, and Cultural Rights: A Textbook, Dordrecht; Boston: Martinus Nijhoff Pub., 1995.

Glenn A. Mower, International Cooperation for Social Justice: Global and Regional Protection of Economic/Social Rights, Westport, Conn: Greenwood Pr., 1985.

Gregory J. Walters, Human Rights in Theory and Practice: A Selected and Annotated Bibliography, Metuchen, NJ: The Scarecrow Press, 1995.

Ian Martin, The New World Order: Opportunity or Threat for Human Rights, Cambridge, MA: Harvard Law School Human Rights Program, 1993.

Jack Tobin and Jennifer Green, Guide to Human Rights Research, Cambridge, MA: Human Rights Program, Harvard Law School, 1994.

Louis B. Sohn, The Human Rights Movement: From Roosevelt's Four Freedoms to the interdependence of Peace, Development and Human Rights, Cambridge, MA: Harvard Law School Human Rights Program, 1995.

Matthew C.R. Craven, The International Covenant on Economic, Social, and Cultural Rights: A Perspective on its Development, Oxford: Clarendon Press; NY: Oxford University Press, 1995.

Nadine Strossen, United States Ratification of the International Bill of Rights: A Fitting Celebration of the Bicentennial of the U.S. Bill of Rights, 24 U. Tol. L. Rev. 203 (1992).

Philip Alston, Making and Breaking Human Rights: the UN's Specialized Agencies and Implementation of the International Covenant on Economic, Social and Cultural Rights, London: Anti-Slavery Society; La Crosse, Wis: National Association of Interdisciplinary Ethnic Studies, (1979).

Rosalyn Higgins, Admissibility Under the Optional Protocol to the International Covenant on Civil and Political Rights, 1991 Can. Hum. Rts. Y.B. 57 (1991).

Scott Davidson, The Inter-American Court of Human Rights, Aldershot, England; Brookfield, VT: Dartmouth Pub. Co. Ltd., 1992.

Scott Leckie, Towards an International Convention on Housing Rights: Options at Habitat II, Washington, DC: American Society of International Law, 1994.

Scott Leckie, When Push Comes to Shove: Forced Evictions and Human Rights, Mexico; Utrecht, Netherlands: Habitat International Coalition, 1995.

Thomas Buergenthal & Harold G. Maier, Public International Law in a Nutshell, St. Paul, MN: West Publishing Co., 1990.

Thomas Buergenthal, International Human Rights in a Nutshell, St. Paul, MN: West Publishing Co., 1995.

Thomas D. Young, International Human Rights: A Selected Bibliography, Los Angeles, CA: Center for the Study of Armament & Disarmament, California State University Los Angeles, 1978.

Torkel Opsahl, The Coexistence Between Geneva and Strasbourg Inter-Relationship of the International Covenant on Civil and Political Rights and the European Convention on Human Rights and Their Respective Organs of Implementation, 1991 Can. Hum. Rts. Y.B. 151 (1991).

Ved P. Nanda, The United States Reservation to the Ban on the Death Penalty for Juvenile Offenders: An Appraisal Under the International Covenant on Civil and Political Rights (Symposium: The Ratification of the International Covenant on Civil and Political Rights), 42 DePaul L. Rev. 1311 (1993).

Walter S. Tarnolpolsky, The Canadian Experience with the International Covenant on Civil and Political Rights Seen from the Perspective of a Former Member of the Human Rights Committee, 20 Akron L. Rev. 611 (1987).

Index

G

H

I

J

M

N

O

P

Q